D1603921

antique
Porcelain Boxes
identification & value guide

Jim & Susan Harran

COLLECTOR BOOKS

A Division of Schroeder Publishing Co., Inc.

Cover design by Terri Hunter
Book design by Erica Weise

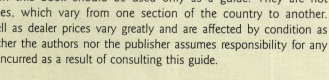

COLLECTOR BOOKS
P.O. Box 3009
Paducah, Kentucky 42002-3009

www.collectorbooks.com

The current values in this book should be used only as a guide. They are not intended to set prices, which vary from one section of the country to another. Auction prices as well as dealer prices vary greatly and are affected by condition as well as demand. Neither the authors nor the publisher assumes responsibility for any losses that might be incurred as a result of consulting this guide.

Proudly printed and bound in the
United States of America

Contents

Dedication

About the Authors

Susan and Jim Harran, antique dealers of A Moment In Time, specialize in English and continental porcelains and antique cups and saucers. The Harrans have authored seven books, entitled *Collectible Cups and Saucers Books I, II, III, and IV; Dresden Porcelain Studios; Meissen Porcelain;* and *Decorative Plates*. They write feature articles for various antique publications. Susan is a member of the Antique Appraisal Association of America Inc., and they are both members of the Antiques & Collectibles Dealer Association. The Harrans do business on the internet. Their website is www.tias.com/stores/amit. The Harrans enjoy traveling around the country to keep abreast of trends in the antiques marketplace. They reside in Neptune, New Jersey.

Acknowledgments

First and foremost, we'd like to thank the staff of Collector Books. If it had not been for our publisher Bill Schroeder, and our editor Gail Ashburn, this book would not have been possible. We appreciate the beautiful cover design by Terri Hunter and the book design by Erica Weise. The staff at Collector Books is professional, talented, and always helpful.

We would like to express our appreciation to those collectors and dealers who so generously gave of their time and knowledge to make this book a reality. We are indebted to our good friend Judy Brim and her mother Helen Foreman of Pryor, Oklahoma, for sending us such excellent quality photographs. Judy has a rare German elfinware collection that she has shared with us through an interview and her wonderful photographs. Thanks for your help and friendship!

A special thank you to Judy Tollefson of Argyle, Texas, for sending us so many photographs from her diverse collection of interesting boxes. Judy is an antique dealer who travels around the world looking for unique items. We especially appreciate her sharing photos of her wonderful figural cat and dog box collection. Thanks for your hard work in making sure the photographs were the best quality.

Once again, we would like to thank Henry Yuen of Toronto, Canada, for sending us so many wonderful photographs of Chinese boxes. Pieces of this quality, age, and condition are rare, and we thank Henry for sharing them with us. Henry wrote a fascinating chapter for our *Collectible Cups & Saucers, Book IV*, entitled "Chinese Tea and Tea Serving Vessels." We have learned much about Chinese porcelains from Henry, and we appreciate his ongoing help.

Thanks again to Joan and Ken Oates from Marshall, Michigan, for sending us photographs from their collection. Joan has written five books on Phoenix Bird China.

Many thanks to our good friend Richard Rendall of Cincinnati, Ohio, for sending us photos from his collection. Thanks to Karen Monday of Butler, Pennsylvania. Karen has a wonderful Dresden collection and contributed many photographs for our book, *Dresden Porcelain Studios*, some of which we were able to use for this book.

Boxes have existed from the time the first person decided to protect his precious belongings and have been made in many different materials. When porcelain making was perfected in Europe in the mid eighteenth century, society became intrigued with porcelain boxes. Artists made them in all shapes and sizes and painted them with great care. The making of these boxes took considerable time and required great skill. The material is well suited for painting, and a number of artists used their talents to make works of art. The variety of a porcelain box collection is only limited by the imagination and budget of the collector.

The purpose of this book is to include information and realistic prices for a wide range of ceramic boxes that are readily found in the marketplace. To our knowledge, there are no other price guides available for boxes of any kind. We have included over 600 color photographs.

Our first chapter includes historical information on early boxes. We discuss the popular snuff box and the quaint habit of snuff taking. We also discuss boxes for beauty, accessory and needlework boxes, medicinal boxes, and writing boxes. We discuss the variety of shapes and subjects that can be found on boxes. We explain how boxes are made and use photographs to illustrate a number of decorative techniques.

Our book is then organized by country or geographic area. The first of these chapters includes information about French boxes, probably some of the world's finest and most eagerly desired. We discuss early faience and soft paste boxes by the famous makers St. Cloud, Chantilly, and Mennecy. We discuss the famous French company Sevres and try to clear up the confusion about the popular "Sevres style" boxes. We discuss early Limoges boxes, and the variety of wonderful boxes made by Paris studios.

In our chapter on German boxes we discuss popular makers of porcelain boxes, including Meissen and Dresden. A growing number of collectors have begun to appreciate the charm and delicacy of elfinware. We discuss this popular novelty and share our interview with elfinware collector Judy Brim from Pryor, Oklahoma. Finally, we discuss Victorian trinket boxes and fairings.

In our chapter on other European boxes, we discuss those made by Royal Vienna, Royal Vienna style, Capodimonte style, Herend, Royal Copenhagen, and Russian boxes.

Our chapter on English boxes includes Staffordshire hen boxes, majolica, parian ware, and information on pot lids. We discuss popular English makers of porcelain boxes, including Coalport, Royal Crown Derby, Irish Belleek, Wedgwood, and Royal Worcester.

Our chapter on Asian boxes includes the early development of porcelain in China and Japan. We discuss Chinese export boxes and other interesting examples from the nineteenth and twentieth centuries, such as hair glue and seal paste boxes. We include examples of Banko, Imari, Kutani, Nippon, and Satsuma boxes.

Some of the most popular boxes collected today are contemporary Limoges boxes made by Artoria, Chamart, Rochard, and Le Tallec. We include photographs from our own personal Limoges collection.

Our last chapter provides useful information for the collector. We include a helpful marks section and an index.

Many publications and the internet have supplied helpful information, and these sources are acknowledged in the bibliography. We hope this book will make it easier for the beginning, as well as the advanced collector, dealer, and appraiser to identify and price porcelain boxes. We realize that in a book of this nature and scope, some degree of error is unavoidable, and we apologize in advance.

We would appreciate hearing your comments, and our address is below. If you would like a reply, please include a self-addressed stamped envelop.

Jim and Susan Harran
208 Hemlock Drive
Neptune, NJ 07753

Background

HISTORY OF BOXES

"The box has been used to protect, contain, or simply to decorate, for centuries...It has been made of every possible material and in every decorative style in history. Beautiful boxes, perhaps more than any other small decorative antiques, have been preserved and collected."

(Klamkin, Marion, The Collector's Book of Boxes)

Boxes have existed from the time the first person decided to protect his precious belongings. In Ancient Greece a large number of boxes in various shapes were discovered in Tutankhamen's tomb. Cosmetic boxes with mirrors, game boxes, and a jeweled double box were found. Small boxes known as *pyxides* were used to store salves and toiletries. In 2500 BC terra cotta boxes were made in India.

When porcelain making was perfected in Europe in the mid-eighteenth century, society became intrigued with porcelain boxes. Artists made them in all shapes and sizes and painted them with great care. The making of these boxes took considerable time and required great skill. The material is well suited for painting, and a number of artists used their talents to make works of art. The variety of a porcelain box collection is only limited by the imagination and budget of the collector.

The porcelain boxes served many functions. They were intended as gifts, as tokens of social or political status, as mementos of loved ones, and as souvenirs of places visited or special events. Many examples of eighteenth and ninteenth century boxes can be found in museums all over the world. "Boxes can be thought of as a window to view society. These objects allow us to experience the fashions and customs of other periods." (*Limoges Boxes* by Faye Stumpf.)

TYPES OF BOXES

TOBACCO BOXES

Tobacco was first introduced to Europe in 1565. Containers were needed to store and properly maintain tobacco. The earliest tobacco box in England belonged to Sir Walter Raleigh in the late sixteenth century. It was cylindrical and seven inches in diameter. The outside was gilt leather. The inside held a glass or metal container to store the tobacco.

Tobacco boxes were also made of salt-glazed stoneware, faience, and blue Delft earthenware. Some of the makers were Mettloch, Delft, Doulton, Wedgwood, and many English companies located in Staffordshire, England.

Snuff Boxes
The Quaint Habit of Snuff Taking

Sniffing tobacco in powder form is as old a habit as smoking. A Franciscan friar, Romano Pane, who went with Christopher Columbus

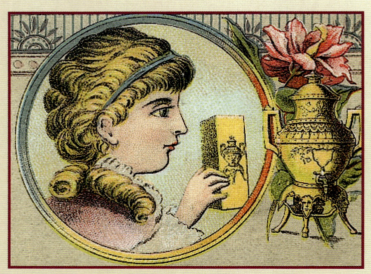

Box with hand-painted flower urn. Trade card Dilworth's Coffee, Ketterlinus, PA.

CATHERINE DE MEDICIS

Catherine de Medici, the first woman to take snuff. French postcard.

on one of his voyages to the New World at the end of the fifteenth century recorded the strange custom of the Indians who ground a golden leaf and sniffed the resulting powder. He reported that they sniffed this strange powder through a y-shaped cane. The lower end was inserted in the powder and the two upper ends in the nostrils.

This golden leaf, or tobacco as it became known, appeared in Europe in the sixteenth century. Fernando Hernandez, a physician and naturalist, was sent by Philip II of Spain to Mexico to investigate the natural resources of the country. He brought back the leaves and seeds of the tobacco plant.

In 1560 the French ambassador to Lisbon, Jean Nicot (from whose name the word "nicotine" is derived) sent some leaves to the French Queen Catherine de Medici, with instructions on how to use snuff to cure her migraine headaches. She became the first woman in Europe to take snuff.

Snuff taking was established in Europe by the mid-sixteenth century although it was often regarded as a disgusting practice. In Russia Tsar Michael decreed that persons convicted of snuff taking should have their noses cut off for their second offense.

During the late sixteenth and early seventeenth centuries, opposition to its use continued to be heard. During the reign of Louis XIII of France, his minister Cardinal Richelieu imposed a tax on tobacco, which later helped the king finance his military campaign. In England in 1584 Queen Elizabeth issued a decree against the misuse of tobacco.

Despite opposition, snuff increased in popularity. At first it was thought to have medicinal powers. Scotch snuff was considered a cure for a great variety of ailments ranging from migraine to the plague. Mr. Payne, located at the Angel and Crown in St. Paul's churchyard, offered his snuff at three shillings, six pence a bottle "as an assured cure for leanness."

Before long it was used for the enjoyment it provided, and in many cases it became a habit. During the reign of Queen Anne (1702 – 1714), there was a great rise in popularity of snuff taking in England. The introduction of coffeehouses contributed to the fashionableness of snuff taking. By the eighteenth century there were 3,000 coffeehouses in London alone. A visitor said of one coffeehouse, frequented by fops, that the closing of their snuff box lids made more noise than their tongues.

The habit became universal in the eighteenth century with over 7,000 shops in London where snuff was sold. It became acceptable in the best of circles, where an elaborate ritual evolved for taking it. While most snuff-users simply helped themselves to a pinch of snuff, the more elegant used tiny spoons made of extremely thin silver. These were only 2" to 2½" in length and were made in all the flatware patterns of the day.

Snuff was always taken into the nostrils with a breath of air. The resulting sneezing required the user to have a handkerchief handy. These were usually snuff brown in color so they would not show the discoloration.

These elaborate and often foolish rituals gave satirists of the day much fuel for their pens. One writer claimed that at church, no one could hear the sermon. "The priest's voice was totally drowned by

"These Lovely Habits." Man putting snuff in his nostrils. Postcard, AH Co.

the noise of the snuff-takers, as they first tapped the lids of their boxes to dislodge any loose grains, followed by the loud 'sniffs' of inhalation, and finally the inevitable sneezes." (*Collecting Small Silverware* by Stephen Helliwell.)

Ladies who took snuff were particularly scorned, with complaints that even the strongest perfumes couldn't disguise the ever-present tobacco odor. Despite the criticism, women continued to indulge in snuff for many years. In the late eighteenth century many women had special pockets sewn inside their gowns to hold dainty snuffboxes close to the warmth of their bodies. This gentle heat was supposed to bring out the aromatic bouquet.

Little girl taking snuff.
French postcard, VIII, C. Clayette, Photographer.

The most hearty snuff taker was Queen Charlotte, the wife of George III. Her excessive indulgence earned her the nickname "Snuffy Charlotte," and her family affectionately called her "Old Snuffy."

King George IV took to the habit with enthusiasm. He changed his snuff according to the time of day. One room in each palace was set aside for the storage of his snuff.

Charles Lamb's sister, Mary, had a passion for snuff taking. Because her use often exceeded what she could afford, she had a rather devious method of getting more. Once a week Miss Lamb did her social rounds, calling on various friends for a cup of tea. She carried in her bag at least a dozen empty snuffboxes. On each call she would take out a box and pretend surprise that it was empty. The hostess would insist on filling the box from her own supply. By the end of the morning a week's supply had been gathered.

One of the most excessive snuff takers was a Mrs. Margaret Thomson of Boyle Street in East London who died on April 2, 1776. She instructed in her will that her coffin containing her body was to be filled with the best Scotch snuff, making it the world's largest snuffbox. Her faithful servant was asked to follow the funeral procession and drop a liberal handful of snuff each 20 yards in the street for the crowd.

By the 1850s cigars and cigar divans were introduced. Cigar divans were tobacco shops that provided comfortable rooms where customers could converse and smoke cigars. During the Victorian era women began to regard snuff taking as demeaning, a habit fit only for the lower classes.

As if to hasten the decline of snuff taking, a Professor Uyr published a widely read report stating that most snuff contained starch, cereals, sawdust, ground glass, lead oxide, rhubarb leaves colored with burnt sienna and made pungent with ammonia.

King George IV. Postcard, Raphael Tuck & Sons, King & Queen of England Series 616.

*Little boy giving snuff to
Man in the Moon, early postcard.*

*"Come and have a pinch of snuff. I've some really splendid stuff."
Postcard, FAS 09241/4.*

The decline was further hastened when both Queen Victoria and the Duke of Wellington condemned the habit in public. By the mid-nineteenth century snuff taking became a much despised and old-fashioned pastime.

The practice of snuff taking is still used today, however, and we often don't know it. Workers in laboratories, ammunition plants, gas companies, and mines, where it would be hazardous to light up, sometimes use it. It is also popular with sportsmen, farmers, and construction workers.

The tobacco from which snuff is made is imported from different parts of the world, such as southern United States, Brazil, Africa, and India. Most of the snuff imported to the United States and England is made in Bavaria, Germany. There the old methods of snuff making are still used.

The process of making snuff is a complicated one. Snuff begins as

a mixture of different kinds of tobacco that are carefully selected and blended. The leaves are fermented in any one of a number of different ways. The leaves are dried, ground, sieved, and then aged in oak barrels like a fine wine to develop the bouquet. The aging may take a year to complete. Then the snuff is flavored with herbs or oils, such as peppermint, bergamot, lavender, or orange blossom.

A notable snuff shop in London which still remains is G. Smith & Sons, the Snuff Centre, at Charing Cross Road, established in 1869. Their business today is brisk with exports to private customers all over the world.

Snuff Boxes Appeal to a Wide Variety of Collectors
The habit of snuff taking was established in Europe by the mid-sixteenth century. Although at first snuff was probably stored

in containers similar to gunpowder flasks, by the middle of the seventeenth century, Europeans found it convenient to carry their snuff in small flat boxes in their pockets. By the end of the eighteenth century snuff taking became widespread among all classes, and boxes were produced in a wide variety of materials to suit people from all walks of life.

One of the joys of collecting snuff boxes is the tremendous variety not only of materials but of shapes, sizes, and decoration. History buffs can find snuffboxes with historical scenes or portraits of famous people. Miniatures enthusiasts can find snuffboxes as small as one inch long. The person who enjoys art objects can seek exquisitely hand-painted and raised gilt porcelain boxes that are true works of art.

Eighteenth century French faience snuff box, Lille, France.

*Portrait of Napoleon I, German postcard,
Stengel & Co., Dresden 29182.*

Some of the finest boxes of the eighteenth century were the beautifully decorated porcelain boxes produced in France and Germany. The early eighteenth century boxes were usually rectangular or oval in shape. Soon the corners were rounded, and the edges were softened by the use of elaborate moldings. These early boxes were rather shallow, since snuff was expensive, and the box was likely to come open and spill the contents. It was in order to prevent this sort of accident that such care was lavished on the construction of the hinge.

Collecting these exquisite boxes became a status symbol. Madame de Pompadour (1721 – 1764) owned 47 examples. A very ornate snuff box set with jewels and bearing the King's portrait was the standard royal present to an ambassador or a visiting prince in the seventeenth and eighteenth centuries. Napoleon had a snuff box for every day of the year.

Collette d'Arville, a French opera singer of the 1930s had an extensive collection of eighteenth century snuff boxes. She is reported to have said, "A snuff box is like a thoroughbred animal. An authentic pedigree increases its value, especially if it can be connected to a famous historical figure."

Cigarette Boxes
Cigarettes weren't produced until about 1850. Since that time decorative cigarette boxes have been made by almost every porcelain manufacturer. Often they were made in dinnerware patterns and could be set on the table with dessert and coffee or displayed in the living room for guests.

SWEETMEAT BOXES
Sweetmeats were items made from sugar. The term came into being in 1456 when sugar was imported into England. In 1490 comfit boxes were made to hold small bits of fruit, nuts, or seeds preserved in sugar. These were enjoyed as a quick snack or as a breath freshener. Shakespeare called them "kissing comfits." A drageoir box was a container for dragees, a type of sweet with aniseed. Louis XIV kept a drageoir box close at hand to cover his bad breath.

A bonbonniere was a container to hold bonbons, and this box originated in France. Small bonbonnieres were carried in a pocket. Larger bonbonnieres were put on a table to hold the candy. Some of these boxes were deeply concave and came in elaborate shapes, such as animals, humans, fruits, vegetables, flowers, shells, and musical instruments. These unusual shapes were referred to as "fantasies." To offer sweets from a bonbonniere, the box was turned upside down as the lid was on the bottom.

"La Bonbonniere." Young man giving his sweetheart a bonbonniere of sweets. French postcard, Leo 190.

Louis XIV. Postcard, Levy et Neurdein Reunis, Paris.

BOXES FOR BEAUTY
Beauty Through the Ages

Every civilization worships beauty and pursues it at enormous expense. Ancient Greek philosopher Sappho said, "What is beautiful is good, and what is good will soon be beautiful." Since early times, women have painted their faces, styled their hair, and perfumed their bodies.

Cosmetics were first used about 40,000 years ago in the border cave region of South Africa. Archaeologists found sticks of red ochre which were used to paint the face and body and were made by mixing iron oxides with animal fat and then heating it to intensify the color.

Make-up was an advanced art by the time of the ancient Egyptians. A 3,000 year old moisturizer made of animal fat and perfumed resin was found in King Tutankhamen's tomb. Egyptian women used a cleansing cream made from oil, lime, and perfume and rubbed oil on

French figural bonbonniere, eighteenth century, shepherd playing flute with dog and two sheep beside him.

their body to combat the drying effects of the sun. They developed the art of decorating eyes by darkening lashes and eyelids with kohl — a mixture of malachite or galena mixed with oil. Eye paint not only made the eyes attractive but helped to ward off flies. All these ingredients were stored in boxes.

In China and Japan women have used white face paint and red rouge and nail coloring for centuries. In Japan women applied a thick chalky powder made from rice flour called *oshiroi* to their skins. They used a rouge made from the extract of safflower called *veni*.

Dressing Table Sets Are Functional and Decorative
Dressing table sets to store cosmetics became fashionable in the eighteenth century and have remained in use today. Many of these sets were decorative as well as useful, and collectors eagerly search for them. A variety of boxes might grace the top of a Victorian lady's dressing table, and all are interesting and have historic significance.

Essential items for the dressing table were powder boxes. These were made by many porcelain makers, and those made by Meissen and the Dresden decorators are especially collectible. Powder boxes are often collected alone, especially figurals in the form of ballet dancers or half dolls. Beginning around 1870 a woman could wear powder without being considered a hussy, and these dainty boxes were made in large quantities. A few of them can be found with the tiny puff, made of fibers or cotton with a tiny handle sticking up.

Rouge boxes are smaller than powder boxes and can be hinged or made into two parts. Because they are small, rouge boxes fit well into a box collection and are eagerly sought by collectors.

One of the largest and most ornate containers found on a dressing table is a trinket box. These were used to hold buttons, cufflinks, odd pieces of jewelry, or small souvenirs and were made by Limoges, Capodimonte, and other European and Oriental porcelain companies. Some were hand painted with flowers, designs, and portraits and were lined with colored plush or velvet. The more elaborate boxes had interior divisions and trays. From 1860 to 1890 porcelain trinket boxes with elaborate lids to decorate the top of a bureau and fairings were imported from Germany in great number.

Some early jewelry boxes are called caskets, and these are very rare. Caskets are usually quite large and hinged, some with bronze stands. The most desirable were those made by Sevres in the eighteenth century.

A young girl powdering face.
Italian postcard,
Visto Revisione Stamps #1354, Milan.

WILL THINK ME BEAUTIFUL?
Me trouvera-t-il belle?

"Will think me beautiful?
Postcard, Selco, Dolly-Series.

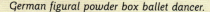

German figural powder box ballet dancer.

Jewelry caskets were used by French ladies as a ploy to add to their jewelry collection. When their lovers were in the bedroom, the ladies would hint about how empty their jewelry box was. Hopefully the next time the lover visited, he would bring a piece of jewelry to make his lady grateful.

Hair receivers are beautiful treasures from a bygone era, and collectors eagerly seek them. They are similar to powder boxes but have an opening in the lid. They were used to hold long strands of hair retrieved from a comb or brush, which were wound around the fingers and inserted into the opening. The saved hair was later woven, braided, or glued into jewelry to be worn during periods of mourning.

All hair receivers have common features that make them easily recognizable. They are usually round, 3" – 4½" diameter, and stand 2" – 2¾" h. The hair receiver has two parts — a base and a lid. There is always a hole in the middle of the lid measuring 1" – 1¾". Many porcelain companies made hair receivers, and those made by Limoges, RS Prussia, and Nippon are especially in demand.

Comment faire autrement que vous chérir toujours Vous qui m'avez offert cet écrin de velours.

Lady showing off jewelry box. French postcard, 1909, BBM #26.

"To my Best Love." Little girl taking necklace out of jewelry box. Postcard, Int. Art Pub. Co., Philadelphia.

Patch Boxes

The outbreak of smallpox in Europe resulted in a curious form of cosmetic. Tiny silk or taffeta cut-outs of dots and other shapes such as stars were applied to the face to conceal smallpox scars. The patches or *mouches* were also worn by wealthy women to draw attention to a pleasing facial feature.

Special boxes to contain the patches were produced in circular, oval, or oblong shapes, similar to snuff boxes but shallower. They were elaborately decorated. Late eighteenth century examples were intricately fitted with tiny compartments for the different patch shapes, a small pot of gum, and a special brush to apply the patch. Some examples may be found with a mirror set into the lid. Smallpox vaccination caused a decline of the disease, and the wearing of patches and beauty spots by both sexes went out of fashion by the beginning of the nineteenth century.

ACCESSORY/NEEDLEWORK BOXES

Created with great imagination by the top jewelers of the day, etuis are delightful objects that have been collected for two centuries. Etuis are small ornamental cases or boxes designed to contain personal articles, such as sewing tools. They are usually cylindrical or rectangular in shape, sometimes tapering slightly toward the bottom. The tops are either hinged or fitted closely over the open end. Later examples are smaller and made to be slipped into a man or woman's pocket or fitted with a ring for suspension from a chatelaine.

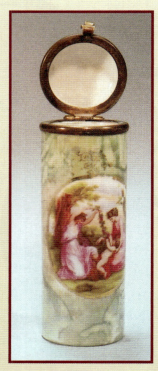

Etui, French or German, transfer decoration.

Similar items, necessaries, are small compartmentalized caskets or containers to store personal items. Necessaries can be found in a variety of shapes, including bird and animal figurals. When displayed in a cabinet or on a table, they are miniature works of art.

Etuis and necessaries were in use from the seventeenth century on, but the more collectible varieties were popular in the eighteenth and early nineteenth centuries when they were considered important objets de vertu (small objects of fine workmanship). They were fashionable gifts throughout Europe, and today examples can be found with presentation inscriptions that add historical interest. One of the finest collections of Georgian etuis was owned by Mary of Teck, wife of George V of Great Britain, king from 1910 to 1936.

The variety of tools and personal items found in etuis and necessaries is quite amazing. Young ladies throughout the nineteenth century wore sewing etuis that hung from a chatelaine. The tools might consist of tiny French or Sheffield-plated scissors with point-protectors, needles, silver thimbles in velvet cases, rulers, and intricately decorated knives called bodkins to punch holes in lacework and double as letter openers.

For the health conscious, an etui might include an ear pick, ear cleaner cup, toothpick, tongue scraper, tiny pill box, and tweezers. The traveling surgeon might carry an etui fitted with several razor-sharp bleeding knives, the steel blades of which folded into tortoiseshell or mother-of-pearl handles. Today it is rare to find an etui complete with all the fittings. Most have several gaps or are totally empty.

A souvenir (French for memory) etui is a flat, rectangular container with a hinged lid. The inside is filled with ivory leaves for notes and a pencil. The souvenir etui was used for writing down notes, such as appointments. Madame de Pompadour had eight souvenir etuis.

MUSÉE DU LOUVRE. — École Française
Maurice-Quentin DE LA TOUR
Portrait de Mme de Pompadour

1049

Portrait of Madame de Pompadour. French post-card, Louvre Museum, Maurice-Quentin de la tour, ND#1049.

A *carnet de bal* which is French for dance notebook is similar to the souvenir etui. It is a beautifully decorated box also with ivory pages and a pencil used by ladies to list their dance partners at a ball.

A bodkin case is a tubular-shaped box with a slip-on lid and rounded ends. This was used in the eighteenth century to hold needles.

A variety of interesting needlework boxes were made from the eighteenth century onwards. Early pins and needles were handmade and scarce and needed a safe container for storage. The eighteenth century needlework box usually contained needles, thread, and tools for sewing.

Lady sewing with needlework box on table. Postcard, French thread box label, c. 1880 – 1890, Photo Martin Breese©️ Retrograph Archive, London.

MEDICINAL BOXES

Pomanders

A pomade box or pomander was a container for aromatic substances and perfumes to ward off contagious diseases and to sweeten the atmosphere. Pomaders were made in Europe from the Middle Ages to the mid-seventeenth century. The side or top of the box was pierced to allow perfume to escape.

Vinaigrettes

Pomade boxes were reintroduced in the eighteenth century as vinaigrettes. Despite the French name, they were an English invention. They were carried by both men and women to prevent infections or to mask unpleasant odors. The inner part of the container was heavily gilded to prevent corrosion. A piece of sponge soaked in aromatic vinegar was placed inside and held in position by the perforated grill.

In the early nineteenth century the vinaigrette contained a blend of smelling salts used by ladies to ward off attacks of the "vapors." Vinaigrettes were often exchanged as tokens of affection and became increasingly decorative.

Pill Boxes

Small circular or oblong boxes to hold pills were a popular form of objet de vertu in the eighteenth or nineteenth centuries and were found in porcelain. Lids were hinged or completely detached. Pocket pill boxes went out of fashion in the late nineteenth century.

WRITING BOXES

Writing boxes were large boxes made to hold ink, an inkpot, pounce box, seal, paper, pencils, and erasers. Many were made of wood and lacquer, but some were also made from porcelain.

Pounce Box

A pounce box is a domed box with a pierced lid. It contained pounce powder which was a fine sand or compound of powdered pumice or resin which was sprinkled on writing paper to prevent ink from smearing. Pounce boxes were made in novelty shapes, such as animals, houses, windmills, or birds. As writing paper improved and with the advent of the blotter in the late nineteenth century, pounce boxes disappeared.

Seal Box

People sealed their letters with a special wafer or seal. Small boxes to contain these wafers were made from the sixteenth to mid-nineteenth centuries. The wafer was made of a dried paste of flour or gelatin and some coloring.

Stamp Box

In the nineteenth century stamp boxes replaced the seal box. The stamp box had a sloping bottom which made the removal of the stamp easier. It sometimes had two or three partitions. These were popular from 1840 to 1910. Entire porcelain desk sets were made with matching decoration. They are very desirable with collectors and included letter boxes, blotters, stamp boxes, and ink containers.

Dresden stamp box decorated by Richard Wehsner, c. 1890s, three slanted compartments for stamps.

SHAPES

Porcelain boxes were made in a variety of interesting shapes. Sizes varied from a small one-inch wide pill box to a large 10" – 12" jewelry casket.

Book shaped boxes were popular around 1710. Then came circular, oblong, and double boxes. During the classical revival of the first quarter of the eighteenth century, after the discovery of Pompeii and Herculaneum, shell and cartouche shaped boxes were made.

Round, oval, and barrel shaped boxes were predominant in the 1740 – 50s. Boxes were also found in diamond, trefoil, quatrefoil, square, and kidney shapes.

Deep oblong or rectangular à cage boxes were made during the 1760 – 1770s. Gold or bronze frames were made to hold porcelain plaques. Meissen and Sevres made many of these à cage boxes, and they are extremely rare today.

Figural boxes are some of the most eagerly collected today. Most bon-bonnieres were made in a variety of interesting shapes. Animal and human forms are especially desirable with collectors. Turtle boxes were made in the late 1800s by Limoges and Dresden decorators. Sentimental heart-shaped boxes were very popular during Victorian times. Other interesting figurals are shoes, vinaigrettes, eggs, and bellows.

Paris heart-shaped trinket box decorated by Bourdois & Bloch, c. 1890 – 1900.

Chantilly was known for producing humorous figural snuff boxes and bonbonnieres, including a lady sitting on a chamber pot and a couple lying in bed. These were copied by Samson in the nineteenth century. Boxes in the form of a cat's or dog's head bring high prices today.

Limoges figural box in form of turtle, decorated by Tresseman & Vogt, c. 1892 – 1907.

French bellows-shaped snuff box decorated by Ruh-Le Prince, Paris, c. 1890s.

Figural French snuff box of a cat head, c. 1830 – 1870.

The clasp to open a hinged box was often a figural as well. Limoges and Paris boxes had clasps in the form of birds, butterflies, elephants, and flowers. A box made by Raymond Limoges, c. 1860s, had a clasp in the form of a horseshoe and tools. Contemporary Limoges boxes almost always have a figural clasp. The clasp usually relates to the subject of the box. For example the clasp on a Rochard bowl of fruit box is hanging cherries.

SUBJECTS

There are a variety of subjects found on hand-painted porcelain boxes. Top of the line are portrait boxes, and good examples bring high prices at auctions and shows. Some collectors prefer allegorical, courting, or hunting scenes. Landscape paintings, animals, birds, and flowers can be found.

FLOWERS

The most popular subject found on boxes is flowers which appear on more than half of all boxes. If they are not on the lid, flowers will be scattered on the sides or inside the box, arranged in a small bouquet.

The Paris decorators painted boxes with lovely flowers. Samson copied the Oriental style polychrome flowers of Chantilly. Dresser boxes decorated by Dresden and Meissen often had beautifully hand-painted flowers. Herend produced boxes with reticulated chintz style flowers that remain popular today.

WATTEAU COURTING SCENES

Watteau paintings portray figures, usually a man and woman, in a landscape or garden setting. These decorations were copied from originals by eighteenth century French artists, such as François Boucher, Johannes Ridinger, Philips Wouvermen, and Antoine Watteau.

Jean Antoine Watteau (1684 – 1721) was a French rococo artist whose charming graceful paintings show his interest in the theater and ballet. He is best known for his fetes gallante, which are small romantic landscapes with wistful lovers in fancy dress.

Watteau-style painting of a man playing music for two ladies in fancy dress, landscape scene. Postcard, Artist Nicolaus Lancret, Stengel & Co., Dresden #29912.

Many Paris decorated boxes can be found with courting scenes, including those done in monochromes (a single color). Sevres style casket boxes are sure to contain courting scenes. Ambrosius Lamm, a Dresden decorator, did a series of small rouge boxes with gold courting scenes on richly colored grounds.

LANDSCAPES

Landscape art portrays scenery such as rivers, lakes, mountains, forests, and gardens. At Meissen in the 1730s, porcelain artists experimented with painting European landscapes, based on Dutch engravings, on snuff boxes. Soon the paintings of landscapes, battles, and harbor scenes achieved great popularity. River or port scenes, with ships docked along the banks and merchants peddling their wares, are referred to as harbor scenes. They are tiny paintings with deep perspective. Soon other porcelain manufacturers such as Sevres produced landscape scenes.

ANIMALS

Animals have always been a popular subject on boxes, especially dogs and cats. Pugs were very popular among the English and French aristocracy in the eighteenth and nineteenth centuries. An early St. Cloud box dated 1750 – 1755 has a wonderful portrait of a pug dog. Madame Pompadour had a pug; therefore, they adorned the lid of many French snuff boxes during the eighteenth century.

BIRDS

Birds have long appealed to Chinese and Japanese potters. A favorite mythological bird which appeared frequently on Chinese boxes was the elegant ho ho bird or phoenix which was the symbol of happiness. It has the head of a pheasant, tail of a peacock, and the legs of a stork or crane and symbolizes beauty, rank, and longevity.

White cranes in flight are often the subjects painted on Chinese export, Japanese Satsuma, and Kutani boxes. The crane means good luck and longevity. In Japan peacocks stand for elegance and good fortune and are often found together in designs with the peony flower.

Manchurian crane, Whipsnade Park. Postcard, Photo by F. W. Bond, property of the Zoological Society of London.

PORTRAITS

Boxes with a well painted portrait are always the most expensive as they were painted by well known porcelain artists of the time. The face of a beautiful woman or that of a famous person, such as Napoleon, can show off the painter's artistic skill. Some portraits on early boxes were done in ivory. Many times they were a portrait of the giver of the box. It was given to a loved one before a trip as a reminder. Some boxes had secret compartments to contain a love note.

CUPIDS

Many box artists enjoyed painting Cupids. Many examples can be found with Cupids holding fruit, flowers, and playing musical instruments. They were often portrayed amidst fluffy clouds. Capodimonte style boxes, in particular, had hand-painted Cupids in relief on the lid.

Two Cupids opening box. German postcard, JB & Co.

WORDS AND PHRASES

Souvenir boxes were very popular in the nineteenth century and were often sold in gift shops. Travelers could buy an inexpensive trinket box to take home for a loved one or friend. French boxes can be found with the phrases pensey a moi (Think of me), je t'aime (I love you), and "A friends Gift."

Photo of Elizabeth Vigee Le Brun, famous eighteenth century French portrait painter of ladies of French court. Postcard, Stengel & Co., Dresden #29826.

French patch box, c. 1890s.

HOW BOXES ARE MADE

A DEFINITION OF PORCELAIN

Porcelain is the name originally given to the Chinese ware brought to Europe by the Portuguese and Italian traders returning home with treasures from the Far East. For centuries porcelain was a secret known only to the Chinese. When Marco Polo, the Venetian explorer, returned home from the court of Kublai Khan in the thirteenth century, he named the rare pieces of china he brought home with him *porcelana* because the glassy surface and texture reminded him of a seashell he knew, a cowrie called *porcelli* in Italian. Porcelain is the finest textured of all ceramics which include earthenware, faience, majolica, and stoneware. It is the ultimate in ceramic quality and beauty.

PREPARATION

True, or hard-paste, porcelain is composed principally of feldspar, quartz, and kaolin, which produce a fine clay that is virtually free of impurities. The relative amounts of these three ingredients vary according to the texture that is desired. The more kaolin, the harder the porcelain. Fired at very high temperatures, hard-paste porcelain is characteristically translucent and white, and has great strength and hardness. It is almost always cast in molds. The beauty and decorative potential of the pure white clay more than compensates for the technical problems involved in its production.

The ingredients of porcelain are carefully washed, ground, and pulverized before they are mixed together. Water is then pressed out of the creamy liquid, and this results in a workable clay which can be stored until it is needed.

Molding is ideal for long production runs of objects which have to be identical in form and size and for intricate shapes. When cakes of clay paste are obtained in a workable state, they are ready for molding. After the process is completed, the piece is trimmed and sponged to a smooth finish.

DESIGNING AND MODELING

To create a new box, a designer must first draw each item and establish a design. A mold must then be made before a box can be produced. The modeler must bear in mind that there will be a reduction in size during the bisque firing, so the model must be at least six percent larger than the finished item. The mold is usually made of plaster of Paris or a resin material.

Boxes are actually produced from working molds. These molds are exact copies in the reverse of the original model. Molds must be very dry before they are used, so that the dry plaster wall will quickly absorb moisture from the paste. With a box, a working mold is required for the shape of the top and bottom of the box itself. Slip is used for the adhesive to add any external decoration. Making these separate working molds is a true art requiring great skill. Model and mold making is one of the most important parts of the production process.

BISQUE FIRING

The first firing of a piece is called bisque or biscuit and requires very careful handling. The molded box goes into a kiln and it takes a piece about 30 hours of firing. The piece will reach temperatures as high as 1,750 degrees Fahrenheit. After cooling to room temperature, it is ready for further processing.

GLAZE

The glaze applied to a box serves several purposes. The first is to form a completely impenetrable surface; secondly, to provide durability to the items for long and hard usage; and lastly, to produce the translucency which is characteristic of a fine porcelain box.

Quartz, feldspar, chalk, and dolomite are mixed together to make a creamy liquid called glaze. The ingredients may vary slightly from company to company for the desired effect.

Glaze is applied to a box by dipping it in a vat of the liquid. The bisque piece is very absorbent, and a layer of glaze is built up. The glaze must be of just the right thickness. After glazing, a box is put in a kiln for firing. More firings may be required depending on the quality and degree of painting and gilding desired.

DECORATION

Porcelain may be decorated at a number of stages in its production. Prior to glazing, the bisque ware is often decorated with colored underglazes or stains. The glaze is applied to the bisque and fired at a much lower temperature than the clay body itself. After the ware has been glazed and fired, it is often further decorated with overglaze enamels, metallic lusters, or decals and then fired yet again at an even lower temperature.

HARDWARE

Most of the porcelain boxes made, regardless of their final use, were mounted with a metal hinge and clasp. The clasp was usually done in the same decoration as the box, for example, a box decorated with flowers would have a flower clasp.

A band of metal tied the top and bottom pieces of the porcelain box together. The metals used were gold, silver, copper, and brass, depending on the box and its use. Only the very best boxes were gold mounted; the less expensive metals were used for the cheaper boxes. Goldsmiths were needed to do this work on the mounts of a box because the work was so delicate and sometimes elaborate. A long piece of the desired metal was shaped to fit each box because each box was unique. The piece of metal would be shaped directly onto each box. The whole frame was glued to its specific box adjusted to provide a tight fit.

The whole process of making the top and bottom piece fit perfect was to ensure a tight-fitting closure. Many of the early boxes were made to hold snuff and were carried in a pocket or purse, so it was essential that the box closed tightly or the powdered snuff would come out.

INSPECTION

The final step of the manufacturing process is the inspection. To be acceptable a box must be free of any defects. Although there are inspections along the way, it's very important that a final inspection is completed. When all the processes have been completed with some minor variations depending on the specific manufacturer, we have a beautiful finished box ready for decoration. It takes a group of many talented skilled people working together to produce a beautiful box.

DECORATIVE TECHNIQUES

MOLDED DESIGN

The early forms of decoration were often molded designs or intricate relief decoration. Most Capodimonte style boxes had Cupids or mythological characters, children, or flowers in relief.

Capodimonte style box showing molded Cupids in relief.

Close-up.

HAND PAINTING

A skilled porcelain artist paints a picture on a piece of porcelain in much the same manner as an artist would paint a picture on a canvas. The painting could be any subject of the artist's choosing. The most popular subjects on boxes were courting scene portraits of beautiful women and men in elegant period

Close-up.

Quimper snuff box with roosters.

costume, landscapes, battle scenes, seascapes, animals, geometric designs, and especially flowers.

TRANSFER PRINTING

Transfer printing was introduced in the 1750s to achieve a high level of detail and accuracy as well as to produce a high volume of items with identical patterns at a relatively low cost. Transfer printing involved putting a design on paper, then transferring it to a copper plate. This was accomplished by piercing the paper with small holes to outline the details of the pattern. The paper was then laid on a copper plate, and a fine powder was sprinkled on the surface to make an image. This image was then engraved into the plate by a sharp instrument. Semi-skilled painters could fill in the outline at a fraction of the cost of skilled painters. In the late nineteenth century some trinket boxes, especially souvenir boxes, were transfer decorated so that they could be sold inexpensively.

The decal method is the process of transferring a design or picture from specially prepared paper sheets, which are printed lithographically. When the paper is put in water, the decal will slide off and adhere to an item. This process is done before putting the objects in the kiln. The decal can be left as it is or in some cases enhanced by additional painting.

Close-up.

German rouge box with transfer design.

MONOCHROME ENAMELS

Painting in a single color, such as black, brown, blue, sepia, and gold or different shades of these colors was called monochrome painting. This form was largely used in France and Germany during the eighteenth century. Many early snuff boxes were hand painted with monochrome decoration. The typical subjects were flowers and courting scenes.

Close-up.

*Nineteenth century Limoges box with
brown monochrome courting scene.*

Close-up.

*Eighteenth century
Sevres portrait casket box.*

FLOWER PAINTING

Realistic hand-painted flowers are abundant on porcelain boxes. Flowers were a popular subject in German porcelain since 1740 when a new style of natural flower decoration developed known as *deutsche blumen* or German flowers. The designs for many of these naturalistic flowers were taken from plates in botanical books. During the nineteenth century, the Paris decorators made many lovely boxes with flower decoration.

COURTING SCENES

Courting scenes or Watteau paintings were first used by Meissen and then copied by the Dresden and Paris decorators. Watteau paintings portray figures, usually a man and woman, in a landscape or garden setting.

Close-up.

*Dresden rouge box
with hand-painted courting scene.*

Close-up.

Meissen dresser box, hand-painted flowers.

PORTRAIT PAINTING

Portrait painting was sometimes used as a method of decorating a porcelain box. The face of a beautiful woman was a common subject, although famous men were often used as well. This type of decoration was very expensive to produce and is only found on the best boxes, such as those made by Sevres, Royal Vienna, and Meissen.

GILDING

Gilding is the art of painting with liquid gold, which is used for ornamentation to enhance fine porcelain boxes. Bright liquid gold was used on large areas and also as a cheap method of undercoating for burnished gold. The bright gold is very shiny and bright in appearance and lays on the surface of the porcelain piece even after firing; therefore, it is perfect for lines and scrolls. Special fine brushes made of animal hair were used for this delicate work.

Burnished gold is often called paste gold. It is not as bright and is applied, much heavier to an object and has a satiny finish. Usually the more heavily a piece is gilded, the more attractive it becomes to collectors. Many of the Dresden decorating studios kept their formulas for their gold decoration a secret.

Sevres style snuff box with gilt flowers.

Close-up.

"Jewels" are made by dabbing dots of different colored enameling, richly colored glaze, or gilt on the object to simulate jewels, such as turquoise, rubies, or pearls. Examples of jeweled pieces are highly regarded by collectors today.

Close-up.

Dresden powder box with gold beading and turquoise jewelling.

HEAVY GOLD PASTE

This method of decorating is almost the same as gilding except the gold is the thickness of heavy cream and is applied almost like slip painting. This technique was used on expensive cabinet pieces.

Close-up.

APPLIED FLOWERS

Flowers, leaves, and any decoration that is not molded but made separately and added to an object with slip falls in the category of applied decoration. The naturalistic look of the applied decoration on Meissen pieces is one of its trademarks. Each petal and leaf of a flower is shaped one-at-a-time, then joined together to form a realistic flower. It is then hand painted and applied to the object to be decorated.

Limoges Le Tallec heart-shaped box, heavy gold paste decoration.

Meissen dresser box, applied flowers.

Close-up.

BEADING/JEWELING

Beading is a decorative method of using beads of clay. These beads may be either cast, applied, or embossed. The effect is obtained by applying beads or dots of slip to achieve the desired effect. The beads are fired in a kiln and then enameled or gilded. Beading is found mostly as a trim decoration.

MOSS

The most unique and charming characteristic on many elfinware boxes is the moss or "spinach" that is encrusted. This decoration is similar to a technique used by Bernard Palissy, the early French potter (1510 – 1590). Palissy's ware was encrusted with organic decoration and animals. The elfinware "moss" is a handwhipped coarse, grouty bisque in two shades of green that was probably applied to the piece by a tube — similar to today's cake decorating techniques.

*German elfinware box
with moss decoration.*

*German elfinware box
with moss decoration.*

DECORATIVE CLASP

One type of decoration unique to boxes is a figural clasp. Limoges and Paris boxes had clasps in the form of birds, animals, insects, and flowers. The clasp usually related to the subject of the box.

*Nineteenth century Limoges snuff
box, clasp in shape of bird.*

Close-up.

TAPESTRY

This interesting decoration was made in the late nineteenth century by a few German companies. Royal Bayreuth is well known for their tapestry pieces, especially the rose tapestry pattern. It was made by wrapping the unfired box with a coarse cloth. The piece was then fired. The cloth burned up in the firing, and the tapestry effect remained. Various decoration was added over the glaze, including floral, scenic, and a few rare portraits.

Close-up.

Royal Bayreuth box with tapestry decoration.

French Boxes

EARLY FAIENCE BOXES

Faience is the French word for a tin glazed earthenware that has been produced in France since the sixteenth century. By the mid-eighteenth century small trinket, jewelry, and snuff boxes were being made at manufacturers in Rouen, Nevers, Marseille, Lille, Sceaux, and Quimper. These early boxes are quite rare today.

RICHARD GLOT

A faience factory began in Sceaux, France, in 1748 and underwent many changes in ownership. Richard Glot took over from 1772 to 1795 and produced high quality faience. He made hinged boxes with silver mounts featuring monochrome landscape scenes and flowers.

JACQUE FEBVRIER MANUFACTURING

This company began operation in 1763 in Lille, France. Faience boxes were produced with courting scenes, flowers, and landscape scenes. Often the inside of the box was fully decorated. Some of the boxes were copied in the nineteenth century by Paris decorators.

VEUVE PERRIN

The Veuve Perrin Faience Factory was founded in Marseille c. 1740 – 1795 by Claude Perrin. The company was continued by his widow and son. Some of the boxes have been copied by nineteenth century Paris decorators.

QUIMPER

The colorful folk art designs on Quimper pottery evoke visions of the simple pleasures of the French countryside. Quimper pottery is a French faience made in Quimper, a picturesque seaside town in the province of Brittany, some 400 miles west of Paris.

The history of Quimper pottery is somewhat complex as three different companies manufactured it during its 300 year history. Each company had its own unique style. Decorating Quimper is a true folk art which has been passed down for generations. Breton country life is illustrated by paintings of sturdy peasants in their traditional costumes. Baskets of flowers and birds, especially the French symbol coq or rooster, are popular designs.

EARLY SOFT PASTE PORCELAIN BOXES

Some of the best French boxes were made of soft paste porcelain in the eighteenth century. Soft paste porcelain was an attempt to copy early Chinese porcelain. Glass or glass-like material called frit was added to the clay mixture. Soft paste porcelain was beautiful and had a soft, creamy look. It was impractical, however, because it scratched and broke easily. The glaze of soft paste porcelain usually contained large amounts of lead.

ST. CLOUD

St. Cloud is the second oldest French factory and produced soft paste porcelain since 1693. The company was run by Pierre Chicaneau and his family. It specialized in snuff boxes, cutlery, and cane handles. The wares copied the decoration on Chinese blue and white porcelain and Japanese Kakemon motifs. During the second quarter of the eighteenth century, St. Cloud made many snuff boxes in the form of animals mounted in silver and gold. Its soft paste was a warm ivory color with a glossy glaze and surface pitting. The artists at St. Cloud covered these manufacturing flaws with intricate floral decoration.

CHANTILLY

This soft paste porcelain company was established in 1725 by Louis Henri de Bourbon, the Prince de Condé. His hobby was collecting Asian ceramics, and he wanted a French company so that he could more easily add to his collection. A tin glaze was used on the soft paste porcelain which gave the product a fine white color. The years between 1755 and 1780 were an outstanding period for the company. Snuff boxes are highly prized. Decorative styles were based on Chinese blue and white designs and Japanese Kakemon polychrome flowers.

Figural snuff boxes were made by Chantilly and influenced the designs of French boxes for the next 200 years. The reclining Chinese man snuff box with silver mounts is a popular piece illustrated in books on boxes. In 1740 Chantilly made a soft

Figural snuff box of lady sitting on chamber pot after eighteenth century box by Chantilly, made by Samson, c. 1890 – 1910.

paste box of a sleeping couple which has been reproduced many times. Chantilly was famous for a high heeled shoe snuff box with polychrome enameled flowers. Samson produced many copies of Chantilly and marked his pieces with the red hunting horn mark.

MENNECY

In 1734 Francois Barlin opened a soft paste porcelain manufactory in Paris. In 1748 the factory moved to his estate in Mennecy. Simple vertical ribbed toilet boxes were made at first. Snuff boxes were then produced, often having molded basketweave patterns with floral sprays on a white ground. Some interesting animal figurals were made, such as horses and swans. Often the animal was lying down to streamline the box so it would fit into the owner's pocket easily.

SEVRES

Sevres is the luxury name in French porcelain. The earliest product, a soft paste porcelain which was translucent and flawless, was first made in 1745 at Vincennes under the blessings of Louis XV. By the early 1800s only hard paste porcelains were being made. The background colors were rich and exquisite. *Bleu de roi, bleu turquoise*, and *rose pompadour* were the company's most famous ground colors. The finest artists of the time decorated the elaborately hinged porcelain boxes with portrait, landscape, and floral reserves surrounded by panels of exquisite gilding. Madame de Pompadour, mistress to King Louis XV of France, was deeply involved in porcelain production and was an avid collector. She had a snuff box for every day of the year, and many were made by Sevres.

Sevres made small porcelain plaques with hand-painted decoration. They were used in furniture and for casket and snuff boxes. They were mounted in gold, silver gilt, and bronze. Few Sevres snuff boxes with plaques have survived today as many were taken apart for the gold and silver.

Sevres Manufactory. Postcard, F. F., Paris.

Sevres toilet wares were used to hold cosmetics for the face and hair. Among French royalty the toilette was done in front of friends, attendants, and tradesmen; therefore, it was important for the royal lady to have a beautiful toilet set to display. Cosmetic boxes were sold in large numbers. They were used for face creams and pastes, rouge, and hair pomade. In 1792 a Sevres toilet set designed by Boizet was presented by Louis XVI to his mistress. It has a bleu de roi ground with jewelling. The set contained boxes for cosmetics, washing, eating, writing, and medicinal use.

Sevres also made casket boxes (coffre) which were used for valuables, money, and important papers. These boxes were large, ranging in size from six to fourteen inches long. Small boxes were made for keeping medicinal items such as a root chewed to prevent bad breath or to hold a mixture of opium and honey used to cure a toothache.

The Sevres Manufactory is still in operation today. In 1983 it made limited edition cigarette boxes created by artist Christian Renonciat. One porcelain box was made to look like foam, and the other made to look like carved wood. His specialty was to imitate one material with another.

SEVRES STYLE

It is rare to find an authentic Sevres box in the marketplace today as they are mostly found in museums and private collections. In the mid to late nineteenth century a Sevres style developed in France.

Many boxes were produced by a Limoges or Paris factory and decorated by Paris Studios. Early Sevres snuff boxes, toilet boxes, bonbonnieres, and casket boxes were copied. Some of the boxes are beautifully decorated and bring high prices. One example is a Sevres style casket box dating c 1880 with a shepherd and shepherdess offering a young lamb up to an angel and rectangular landscape panels. This box was valued at a 1991 Sotheby's sale for $1,200 – 1,600.

Other Sevres style boxes are of a lesser quality with simple hand-painted decoration but are still eagerly collected, especially those that are small and hinged. There are copies of snuff boxes, powder boxes, patch boxes, and figural bonbonnieres, and they range in price from $75 to $200. Sevres style boxes often have imitation Sevres marks such as the double L mark, the First Empire mark, and various Chateau marks.

LIMOGES

Limoges is the center of the ceramics industry in France. Limoges is about 200 miles southwest of Paris and owes it prominence in the field of hard paste porcelain production in France to the abundance of

Postcard showing city of Limoges, France. D. B., Shumur.

natural resources. The soil in the area is rich in deposits of kaolin and feldspar, the essential ingredients for hard paste porcelain. Most of the kaolin was supplied to the Sevres Company and Paris based porcelain manufacturers in the late eighteenth and early nineteenth centuries.

By the middle of the nineteenth century, porcelain manufacturers began to flourish in the Limoges area. The period of the mid to late 1800s was the golden age for the Limoges porcelain industry.

Boxes were made in Limoges as early as the twelfth century of cham-plevé enamel work. The first porcelain Limoges boxes appeared in the first part of the nineteenth century. The older boxes were usually shaped as rectangles, ovals, hearts, or eggs and were decorated with flowers, fruit, fish, cherubs, and embellished with gold accents. A Limoges snuff box decorated by Raymond Laporte, c. 1860 – 1870s was shaped like a clamshell. It featured a blacksmith's clasp with floral decoration and is valued in the $150 – 200 range.

Most of the boxes made by the Limoges factories in the nineteenth century were sent to one of the Paris studios for decoration. Because of a large export market in the late 1800s the Limoges factories were busy decorating dinnerware items. Approximately 75% of the dinnerware was exported, the largest percentage to the United States.

Although the Limoges companies didn't decorate many hinged boxes during this period, they did make and decorate many dresser sets as these were very popular during the Victorian era. Limoges dresser items were exported to the United States in great quantities.

Tresseman & Voigt produced many beautiful dresser sets and individual pieces, such as powder boxes, hair receivers, rouge boxes, and matching trays. Sets can be found with flowers, Cupids, and holly. It

The Haviland Porcelain Manufactory, postcard.

was also the largest Limoges producer of blanks, sent to the United States for home decorating. Dresser sets were also made by GDM, La Limousine, GDA, Guerin, Bawo & Dotter, and Haviland.

PARIS PORCELAIN

Paris porcelains are made from hard paste and were made or decorated in and around the city of Paris from 1770s until the late nineteenth century. Some sprung up in the old faience manufacturing district in northeast Paris. Around 1850 there were about 75 decorators in the area. Most of the shops did not make the porcelain but purchased white ware from factories in Limoges.

Most antique snuff boxes found today are likely to be Paris copies of an earlier design made by Sevres, Chantilly, St. Cloud, or Mennecy. These later examples are almost as interesting as the originals made in the eighteenth century. At least half of the boxes had no trademark at all. Others were marked with a phony Sevres mark, and a few had the trademark of the Paris studio that decorated it.

JACOB PETIT
Jacob Petit is one of the best known Paris porcelain decorators. He was trained as a painter and traveled all over Europe visiting porcelain factories and decorating studios before opening up his own porcelain company in 1834 at Rue de Bondy in Paris. A few years later he established a larger factory in Fontainebleau where only ornamental articles were produced. He sold his company to one of his employees in 1862. Jacob Petit was a great designer and drew inspiration from many manufacturers and various periods. His products were quite ornamental and decorative. A box signed Petit (JP) would be rare and quite expensive.

PORCELAIN DE PARIS
This decorating studio was begun at Rue de la Pierre-Leveé in 1773 by Jean Baptiste Locré. Three generations of the Clauss family took over operation beginning in 1829. It went through several changes in management until the Achille Bloch family took over after 1887. The company is still in operation today producing luxury porcelain and expensive table services.

The Porcelain de Paris company made many hinged snuff boxes, etuis, patch boxes, and table boxes. Many are heavily decorated with hand-painted flowers and raised gilt. Some were oval, heart, or cartouche shaped or in the form of musical instruments, bellows, kegs, and shoes. It first copied the marks of other factories, using the crown N back stamp of the Naples factory Capodimonte, interlocking L's of Sevres, and crossed swords emblem of Meissen. It began applying its own marks around 1869.

SAMSON

Edmé Samson began the company Samson, Edmé et Cie in Paris, in 1845. His intent was to make reproductions of early ceramics displayed in museums and private collections. The factory was moved to Montreuil, Seine-Saint-Denis, in 1864 by his son Emile Samson. The company closed in 1969.

The company got inspiration from other factories or directly copied their pieces. They copied Meissen, Sevres, Chelsea, and Derby porcelains, Italian majolica, Persian style items, and Palissy. It made many boxes copied from Chinese famille rose styles between 1720 and 1790 and Japanese Imari wares. It copied the soft paste boxes of St. Cloud and Chantilly, using cream colored earthenware to simulate the soft paste porcelain.

Samson didn't set out to deceive the public with his reproductions and claimed all his products would be distinctly marked to avoid confusion. Later some unscrupulous dealers removed the Samson marks in an attempt to defraud the public.

Samson snuff box, c. 1890s, Oriental style flowers.

Samson mark.

Samson made snuff boxes and patch boxes, copying Chinese Export boxes with armorial themes and polychrome flowers, Chantilly figural boxes, such as a man and woman in bed and a lady on a chamber pot.

PAUL BOCQUILLON

Paul Bocquillon of Faubourg St. Denis, Paris, is not well known now, but he specialized in the reproduction of old china and earthenware in the nineteenth century. He made a variety of hinged boxes, including Capodimonte style and used a gold anchor mark.

FEUILLET OF PARIS

This was a Paris decorating shop located at Rue de la Paix c. 1817 – 1845. Feuillet decorated Sevres blanks in the eighteenth century style. One of his trademarks was encircled L's with an F in the center. He made a variety of hinged boxes.

MANSARD & HOURY

This was a Paris partnership active at the end of the nineteenth century until the early twentieth century. They produced reproductions of Sevres boxes, including some nice quality casket boxes.

POUYAT & RUSSINGER

This partnership was descended from Jean Baptiste Locré's company. Russinger became the sole owner 1787 – 1797 and then brought in Pouyat and Sons c. 1808 – 1825+. The factory produced outstanding porcelain in the Meissen style. Exceptional boxes were produced by this Paris company.

FRENCH ART POTTERY

LONGWY

Longwy Pottery began operation in 1798 and is located in Lorraine, France. In 1875 Emaux de Longwy introduced wares that were decorated with Oriental inspired designs, cloisonné enamels in particular. His designs were outlined in black and then filled in with brilliantly colored glazes, especially the turquoise color for which the pieces are most famous. Examples are marked "LONGWY," either printed under the glaze or impressed. Many Longwy items have a uniform crazing which doesn't take away from the value. Longwy made a variety of dresser boxes in the late nineteenth and early twentieth centuries.

ULYSSE BLOIS

Ulysse Blois revived French faience in the early twentieth century. He was known for his deep Prussian blue glaze. His favorite subjects were a stylized swan with an arrow through its body and a dragon. He manufactured the ware himself in his studio and had a circle of wealthy patrons who encouraged and subsidized his work. Blois made some interesting dresser boxes.

Trinket box.

Blois, Ulysse, French faience, c. 1932.

Two part box, 5" x 2"h.

Special presentation box dated
April 1932, deep Prussian blue glaze
with stylized swan with an arrow
through its body (see mark 4).

$300.00 – 350.00.

Close-up.

Snuff box.

Chantilly, c. 1770 – 1790.

Hinged box, 2¾" x 1¾".

Polychrome enamel flowers (see mark 8).

$400.00 – 500.00.

Snuff box.

Glot, Richard, Sceaux, France, c. 1770s.

Octagon shaped with silver mounts, 2⅛" x 1".

Hand-painted cobalt blue monochrome landscape scenes with a castle on the top of box and on sides.

$300.00 – 350.00.

Close-up of lid showing monochrome painting.

Snuff box.

Glot, Richard, Sceaux, France, c. 1770s.

Hinged faience box, 2½"l x 1½"w x 1"h.

Reddish purple monochrome flowers (see mark 30).

$250.00 – 300.00.

Close-up.

Snuff box.

Jacques Febvrier Manufacturing, Lille, France, 1763.

Faience box, 2¼" x 1½" x 1¼".

Original brass frame; rare tin glazed oxides of manganese, cobalt, vert, umber, and mauve enamels with floral sprays on all surfaces, central heraldic coat of arms on the lid (see mark 28).

$500.00 – 600.00.

Close-up of lid.

Snuff box.

Jacques Febvrier Manufacturing, Lille, France, 1763.

Faience cartouche shaped hinged box, 4" x 2".

Original brass frame; hand-painted lake scene with lovers, artist signed Aubo, hand-painted flowers inside and outside bottom.

$500.00 – 550.00.

Close-up.

Open view.

Bisque figural box.

French bisque, marked depose, c. 1890s.

Adorable baby in a steamer trunk, 6" x 7½" h.

Nice quality baby with a soft pink and white gown and blue and white striped socks sitting in trunk which reads "cabin baggage."

$300.00 – 350.00.

Close-up of baby's face.

Trinket box.

Limoges, Chaufriasse, Marcel, c. 1930s.

Round two part box, 5"d x 1½"h.

Pate-sur-pate design two Cupids, cobalt blue ground (see mark 9).

$275.00 – 300.00.

Close-up of lid.

Pin box.

Limoges, Haviland, c. 1876 – 1930.

Two parts, 3¾" x 2" x 1".

Lovely hand-painted lilacs outlined in gold (see mark 45).

$100.00 – 125.00.

Close-up.

Snuff box.

Limoges, Laporte, Raymond, c. 1860 – 1870s.

Hinged, shaped like a clamshell, 1¾" x ¾".

Original brass frame with blacksmith's clasp with a horseshoe and tools; red and yellow flowers with purple swirls (see mark 47).

$150.00 – 200.00.

Close-up showing unusual clasp.

Snuff box.

Limoges, decorated by Pouyat &
Russinger, Paris, c. 1808 – 1825.

Oval and domed, 1¾" x 1⅓" x 1".

Original brass frame; hand-painted flowers
on a beige ground (see mark 70).

$125.00 – 175.00.

Figural box.

Limoges, T & V, c. 1892 – 1907, made for
Burley & Co., Chicago.

Two part box in form of turtle,
5"l x 1¼"h.

Green with allover gold decoration on
shell, gold head and feet.

$300.00 – 350.00.

Open view.

Trinket box.

Limoges, 1890s.

Hinged box, 2¼"l x 1½"w x 1"h.

Souvenir box with "pensey à moi" or "think of me."

$75.00 – 95.00.

Another view.

Dresser set.

Limoges, T & V, c. 1900.

Set includes tray, footed powder box, hair receiver box, vase, hatpin holder, pin box, and pin tray.

Hand-painted yellow roses, aqua/lavender border on pale yellow ground, gilt embellishments.

$600.00 – 700.00.

Dresser box.

Limoges, T & V, c. 1892 – 1907.

Two part box.

Hand-painted roses, gilt.

$200.00 – 250.00.

Snuff box.

Probably made by Limoges and decorated by a Paris decorator, late nineteenth century.

Oval with a slightly domed lid, hinged, 1¾" x ½" x 1".

Original brass frame; figural clasp in the shape of a bird; hand painted with blue forget-me-not flowers and green dots.

$150.00 – 200.00.

Rouge box.

Limoges or Paris, late ninteenth century, unmarked.

Round box, hinged, 2⅓" x 1⅓"h.

Original brass frame; decorated with hand-painted roses and green and blue leaves in a cross-hatch design.

$100.00 – 125.00.

Patch or pill box.

Made in Limoges and decorated by a Paris studio, c. 1890s.

Hinged round box, 1¼" x ½"h.

Original brass frame; decorated with hand-painted flowers and a message, "Je t'aime" or "I love you."

$75.00 – 95.00.

Patch or pill box.

Made in Limoges and decorated by a Paris studio, c. 1890s.

Hinged round box, 1¼" x ½"h.

Original brass frame; decorated with hand-painted flowers and a message, "Je t'aime" or "I love you."

$75.00 – 95.00.

Etui box.

Made in Limoges and decorated by a Paris studio, c. 1920 – 1930s.

Unusual scroll-shaped hinged box with opening in middle, 5"l x 2½".

Four gold handles; dark blue ground with gold leaves on back, white enameled beads on front, hand-painted flowers.

$100.00 – 125.00.

Open position.

Snuff box.

Made in Limoges decorated by Paris decorator, c. 1890s.

Hinged, brass fittings are original and clasp is in form of a bow, 1¾" x 1"h.

Lid has hand-painted musical instruments and a song book on a blue ground.

$100.00 – 150.00.

Close-up of lid.

Snuff box.

Made in Limoges, Leveille studio, Paris, c. 1850s.

Hinged, shaped somewhat like a heart with a butterfly clasp, 1½" x 1¾" x 1".

Lovely hand-painted winter scene on top, artist signed Mesnier.

$150.00 – 200.00.

Close-up showing butterfly clasp.

Snuff box.

Made in Limoges decorated by Paris decorator, c. 1890s.

Hinged, cartouche-shaped, 2" x 1½" x ½".

Hand-painted brown monochrome courting scenes.

$75.00 – 100.00.

Trinket box.

Limoges, c. 1950s, artist signed S. E. G.

Octagonal hinged box, 2" x 1".

Hand-painted scene of the Arc de Triompe in Paris.

$75.00 – 100.00.

Trinket box.

Limoges, c. 1900.

Hinged box, 3"l x 1"w x ¾".

Hand-painted laurel leaves, gilt.

$95.00 – 115.00.

Ring box.

Limoges, unidentified factory, probably decorated in Paris, c. 1920.

Hinged box, 1¼"w x 1¼"h.

Aqua rose and flowers with gilt.

$75.00 – 95.00.

Figural box.

Limoges, c. 1920s.

Fan shaped hinged box, 2⅔"l x 1¾"w x 1"h.

Rich cobalt blue with hand-painted gilt design.

$75.00 – 95.00.

Figural box.

Limoges, 1920s.

Hinged box in shape of shoe, 3½" x 2".

Hand-painted flowers with gilt buckles, gold flowers inside.

$95.00 – 125.00.

Another view.

Trinket box.

Limoges, c. 1950s.

Hinged box, 5½"l x 3¼"w x 2"h.

Mixed decoration flowers (see mark 56).

$100.00 – 125.00.

Trinket box.

Limoges, unidentified mark, c. 1900 – 1930s.

Cartouche shaped hinged box.

Hand-painted flowers, cobalt border (see mark 55).

$125.00 – 150.00.

Dresser box.

Longwy, France, c. 1920 – 1930s.

Two part box.

Typical floral cloisonné enamel decoration on turquoise blue.

$150.00 – 175.00.

Another view.

Snuff box.

Veuve Perrin, Marseilles, c. 1760.

French faience diamond shaped hinged box, 3" x 1¾" x 1".

Original brass frame; lake scene with houses and sailboats on lid, floral sprays on bottom.

$300.00 – 350.00.

Close-up of lid.

Snuff box.

Veuve Perrin, Marseilles, c. 1760.

French faience hinged box, 2½" x 1¾" x 1¼".

Original brass frame; dark green mono-chrome roses with insects on each side (see mark 103).

$300.00 – 350.00.

Close-up of lid.

Snuff box.

Paris, Bourdois & Bloch, c. 1890 – 1900.

Oval hinged box, 2⅛" x 1½" x 1".

Original brass frame; red-violet purple camaieu landscape scene on lid, flowers on the sides, bottom and inside (see mark 64).

$200.00 – 250.00.

Close-up of lid.

Trinket box.

Paris, Bourdois & Bloch, c. 1900 – 1920.

Hinged box.

Hand-painted courting scene on lid; hand-painted flowers (see mark 66).

$125.00 – 150.00.

Figural box.

Paris, Bourdois & Bloch, c. 1920s.

Barrel or keg shaped hinged box, 3½" x 2⅓".

White with hand-painted roses with gold accents (see mark 67).

$250.00 – 275.00.

Trinket box.

Paris, Bourdois & Bloch, c. 1920s.

Heart-shaped hinged box, bright gold inside, 2⅛" x 2½".

Hand-painted courting scene on lid, gilt decoration with red jewel-like enameling on sides.

$200.00 – 225.00.

Close-up of lid.

Etui.

Paris, Bourdois & Bloch, c. 1890s.

Hinged box, 4½"l x 3½"w x 1½"h.

Hand-painted flowers, raised gold.

$300.00 – 350.00.

Trinket box.

Paris, Bourdois & Bloch, c. 1920s.

Heart-shaped hinged box, 2½"l x 2""w x 1¼"h.

Green ground with hand-painted flowers and gilt.

$125.00 – 150.00.

Trinket box.

Bourdois & Bloch, c. 1890s.

Hinged cartouche shaped, 3½" x 2¼" x 1¼".

Turquoise blue ground with raised gold bell-type designs, courting scene cartouche on lid, three land-scape scenes on bottom sides, hand-painted flowers inside.

$400.00 – 450.00.

Open view.

Close-up.

Trinket box.

Bourdois & Bloch, c. 1890s.

Hinged heart-shaped box, 2⅛" x 1".

Hand-painted flowers on lid, inside, and bottom (see mark 65).

$150.00 – 175.00.

Open view.

Patch box.

Paris, Bloch, Marc Eugen, c. 1868 – 1887.

Hinged box, 2"l x 1½"w x 1"h.

Hand-painted courting scene on lid, enameled flowers on sides.

$200.00 – 250.00.

Trinket box.

Bloch & Cie., Paris, c. 1887 – 1900, artist signed M. Garcia.

Hinged cartouche shaped, 3"w x 3¼"l x 1¼".

Pink ground with raised gold, cartouches with two Cupids on lid, landscapes on sides (see mark 62).

$700.00 – 800.00.

View of clasp and scenic cartouche.

Close-up.

Trinket box.

Paris, Achille Bloch, c. 1920 – 1960.

Hinged, cartouche shaped, 3½" x 3" x 1¼".

White with hand-enameled flowers (see mark 63).

$100.00 – 125.00.

Snuff box.

Paris, Fauboug St. Denis, c. 1830.

Hinged box, 2½" x 2".

Lavender ground with cartouches of hand-painted flowers (see mark 68).

$300.00 – 350.00.

Casket box.

Paris, Milet, Paul & Fils, Sevres mark.

Hinged box, 4½" x 3½".

Rare flambé glaze (see mark 69).

$250.00 – 300.00.

Trinket box.

Paris, Pouyat Brothers, Rue Fontaine-au-Roi, c. 1808 – 1825.

Cartouche-shaped hinged box, 3¾" x 1¾".

Bright yellow, covered with pearl jeweling, gold beads, and raised gilt decoration, courting scene cartouche in center of lid framed by gold (see mark 71).

$500.00 – 550.00.

Open view.

Close-up.

Snuff box.

Paris, Ruh-Leprince, Arnold, c. 1890s.

Bellow-shaped hinged box,
4¼" x 2"w x 1¼"h.

Courting scene on lid, raised gilt
(see mark 72).

$350.00 – 400.00.

Open view.

Snuff box.

Paris, Samson, c. 1890s.

Hinged, 2½" x 1¾" x 1¼".

Original brass frame; decorated with Oriental
style flowers and a purple dot and crosshatch
motif (see mark 76).

$175.00 – 225.00.

Trinket box.

Paris, Samson, c. 1873 – 1876.

Hinged box, 3¼"w x 1¾"h.

Basketweave mold, hand-painted
flowers with gilt trim (see mark 73).

$250.00 – 275.00.

Pill box.

Paris, Samson, c. 1873 – 1876.

Hinged box, 2¼"w x 1¾"h.

Purple dot and crosshatch motif, hand-painted flowers with gilt trim.

$125.00 – 150.00.

Patch box.

Paris, Samson, c. 1876 – 1884.

Round box, 1¼"d.

Purple monochrome courting scene on lid (see mark 74).

$150.00 – 175.00.

Open view.

Close-up of lid.

Snuff box.

Paris, Samson, c. 1876 – 1884.

Replica of early hinged snuff box, 2⅓"l x 1¾"w x 1¼".

Coat of arms and floral decoration.

$150.00 – 175.00.

Close-up.

Figural snuff box.

Paris, Samson, c. 1890 – 1910, after eighteenth century box by Chantilly.

Hinged figural box, 3¼"l x 2⅛"w x 2"h.

Figure of man and woman in bed, beautifully hand painted, polychromed Oriental flowers (see mark 75).

$300.00 – 350.00.

Another view.

Close-up of lid.

Trinket box.

Paris, Samson, c. 1890s.

Quatrefoil-shaped hinged box,

Polychromed enameled flowers in the Oriental style.

$225.00 – 275.00.

Figural snuff box.

Paris, Samson, c. 1890 – 1910, after eighteenth century box by Chantilly.

Hinged figural box of lady sitting on chamber pot, 2¾"w x 3½"h.

Hand-painted (see mark 77).

$250.00 – 300.00.

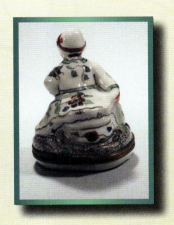

Back of box.

Trinket box.

Paris, Samson, c. 1900.

Hinged box, 4"l x 2½"w x 1¾".

Pink and purple flowers and green leaves with unusual raised white enameled design.

$200.00 – 250.00.

Close-up of lid.

Snuff box.

Paris, Samson, c. 1900.

Hinged box, 2½"l x 1½"w x 2"h.

Copy of eighteenth century Chantilly box, Oriental design with mouse on lid.

$100.00 – 125.00.

Close-up.

Trinket box.

Paris, Samson, c. 1876 – 1884.

Hinged box, 2⅓" x 1¾" x 1¼".

Coat of arms and floral decoration.

$200.00 – 250.00.

Bonbonniere.

Paris studio, c. 1890s.

Hinged with gold knop or finial, figural clasp in the shape of an elephant, 1⅓" x 1½"h.

Original brass frame; black ground with hand-painted flowers on the side and gold decoration on top.

$150.00 – 200.00

Patch box.

Paris, unmarked, c. 1890s.

Hinged, 2¼" x 1".

Sky blue with white jeweling and gold beads along the bottom, the lid has a French city scene.

$60.00 – 75.00.

Trinket box.

Paris, c. 1890s.

Hinged box, 2⅔" x 2".

Hand-painted flowers inside and outside, trimmed with gilt.

$200.00 – 250.00.

Trinket box.

Paris, c. 1900.

Doré bronze oval hinged box, 4¼"w x 3¼"h.

Soft coral ground with jeweled flowers and foliage, wonderful painting of a Russian wolfhound.

$800.00 – 900.00.

Close-up.

Another view.

Trinket box.

Paris, c. 1920s.

Hinged box, 2½"l x 1¼"w x 1"h.

Allover hand-painted floral decoration.

$150.00 – 175.00.

Open view.

Trinket box.

Paris, c. 1890s.

Hinged box, 3"l x 1½"w x 1½"h.

Hand-painted courting scene on lid, flowers inside and out, cobalt ground with raised gold (see mark 78).

$250.00 – 300.00.

Open view.

Trinket box.

Paris, Vielle, France, 364 Rue St. Honore Paris, c. 1890 – 1910.

Hinged box, 5⅛"l x 3½"w x 1½"h.

Turquoise blue with cartouches of hand-painted flowers outside and inside.

$250.00 – 300.00.

Pill box.

Paris, c. 1890s.

Round two part box.

Hand-painted flowers, green border.

$75.00 – 95.00.

Snuff box.

Quimper, unmarked, c. 1760 – 1780.

Cartouche-shaped hinged box, 2¼" x 1".

Original brass frame; hand-painted lid with a colorful rooster or coq perched on a fence, motto, loosely translated, "When will this rooster finish singing to me!"

$300.00 – 350.00.

Another view showing lid.

Snuff box.

Quimper, unmarked, 1760 – 1780.

Octagonal with silver mounts,
2⅞" x 2" x 1¼".

Hand-painted houses on lid, bright yellow
ground, flowers and insects on sides.

$350.00 – 400.00.

Snuff box.

Sevres, c. 1800 – 1810 or earlier.

Diamond-shaped hinged with silver mounts,
3¼" x 2½" x 1¼".

Lid of the box has an amusing motto, roughly translated as
"Note for one hundred kisses — payment on presentation of
the note"; Assignat means the new bank notes during the
French revolution which lasted 8 – 10 years (see mark 97).

$400.00 – 500.00.

Close-up.

Casket box.

Sevres, c. 1772 date mark.

Hinged box, 5"l x 4"w x 2½"h.

Well painted portrait of a French court beauty on lid, pink ground, hand-painted flowers, gold beads, and heavy gold paste decoration, including a crown and fleur-di-lis crest mark on front of box (see mark 96).

$1,800.00 – 2,000.00.

Another view.

Snuff box.

Sevres, c. 1850s, artist signed.

Lyre-shaped hinged box, 4"l x 3¼"w x 1⅓"h.

Pale pink ground, raised gold flowers and scrolls, hand-painted portrait of man playing lute and landscape scene on lid.

$600.00 – 695.00.

Close-up of lid.

Open view.

Snuff box.

Sevres, c. 1804 – 1809.

Hinged box, 2¾" x 1¾".

Apple green crisscross marks with raised gold roses and decoration in between, crest of Napoleon on lid.

$250.00 – 300.00.

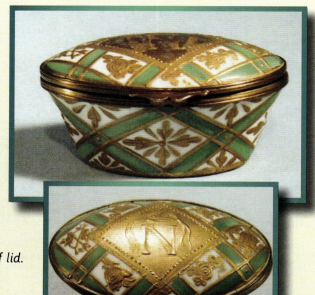

Close-up of lid.

Etui box.

Sevres, c. 1804 – 1809.

Hinged box, 4¼"h.

Green ground with raised gold paste decoration, gold eagle perched on an urn on front.

$350.00 – 400.00.

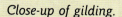

Close-up of gilding.

Portrait box.

Sevres, c. 1804 – 1809, artist signed Dais.

Round hinged box, 3⅓".

Hand-painted portrait of Napoleon framed by ornate gold paste on lid, two floral cartouches on the sides, and flowers on inside, burnt orange ground (see mark 98).

$800.00 – 900.00.

Close-up.

Open view.

Trinket box.

Sevres, c. 1870s.

Unusual kidney shaped hinged box, 3¾"w x 1½"h.

Hand-painted cupids and eagle on lid, done in French technique called en-grasielle or shades of gray, dark red ground with raised gold.

$500.00 – 550.00.

Close-up of lid.

Snuff box.

Serves style, probably made in Paris, c. 1870 – 1890s.

Trefoil shaped, hinged, 2¼" x 2" x 1".

Original brass frame; decorated with hand-painted gold flowers on the lid and inside with a leafy garland on the side (see mark 92).

$300.00 – 350.00.

Bonbonniere.

Sevres style, probably decorated by a Paris studio, c. 1890s.

Quatrefoil shaped, hinged, 2" x 1½" x 1¾".

Original brass frame; used for bonbon candies, hand-painted flowers with gilt trim on lid, black ground.

$125.00 – 150.00.

Trinket box.

Serves style, c. 1850s.

Quatrefoil hinged box.

Hand-painted flowers, blue fleur-de-lis decoration with raised (see mark 90).

$400.00 – 450.00.

Trinket box.

Sevres style, c. 1850s.

Quatrefoil hinged box.

Hand-painted flowers, blue border with gold decoration.

$300.00 – 350.00.

Close-up.

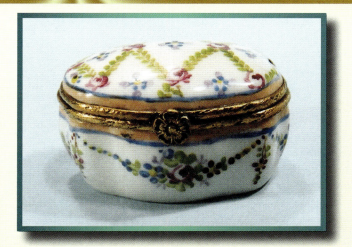

Trinket box.

Sevres style, c. 1890.

Hinged with flower clasp, 2" x 1½".

Hand-painted flowers framed by green ferns (see mark 95).

$150.00 – 175.00.

Trinket box.

Sevres style, c. 1820 – 1850.

Hinged box, 3"l x 2¼"w x 1 ½"h.

Hand-painted courting scene on lid and all sides of box, turquoise ground with raised gold.

$250.00 – 300.00.

Close-up.

End view.

Patch box.

Sevres style, c. 1900 – 1910.

Round hinged box, 2½" x 1½".

Pink ground with hand-painted roses and gilt.

$75.00 – 95.00.

Casket box.

Sevres style, c. 1890s, artist signed M. Leras.

Large octagonal hinged box, 7¼" x 2"h.

Courting scene on lid, lamb on side, hand-painted flowers inside, cobalt with raised gold decoration (see mark 94).

$400.00 – 450.00.

Close-up of lid.

Patch box.

Sevres style, c. 1880s.

Hinged box, 1¾".

Gilt eagle perched on arrows on lid, gilt leaves on sides.

$75.00 – 100.00.

Trinket box.

Sevres style, c. 1880 – 1890s.

Heart-shaped hinged box, 2".

Celeste blue ground, cartouche of hand-painted flowers on lid (see mark 93).

$115.00 – 125.00.

Casket box.

Sevres style, c. 1870 – 1890, artist signed
M. Alaminos.

Blown out hinged box, 10"l x 6¼"w x 3"h.

Rich cobalt blue with raised gold paste decoration, courting scene on lid, scenic cartouches
on sides.

$1,000.00 – 1,200.00.

Open view.

Close-up of lid.

Casket box.

Sevres style, c. 1870 – 1890, artist signed Garnier.

Hinged box with four curved gold feet,
7"l x 4½"w x 4"h.

Cobalt blue with raised gold paste decoration, hand-
painted lovers with lamb and dog on lid, four cartouches of gold flowers and torches on sides.

$800.00 – 900.00.

Close-up of lid.

Casket box.

Sevres style, c. 1870 – 1890.

Hinged box, 6"l x 2½".

Cobalt blue ground with gilt musical instruments and roses.

$350.00 – 400.00.

Close-up of lid.

Trinket box.

Sevres style, c. 1890s.

Navette-shaped hinged box, 4½" x 1½".

Burgundy red with floral reserve, pearl enameling and gilt.

$200.00 – 250.00.

Trinket box.

Sevres style, c. 1900 – 1920.

Hinged box.

Hand-painted roses framed by cobalt blue lines and dots.

$125.00 – 150.00.

Casket box.

Sevres style, c. 1870 – 1890.

Hinged box.

Hand-painted roses and green ferns, cobalt and gilt decoration.

$200.00 – 250.00.

Portrait box.

Sevres style, c. 1850 –1870s.

Bronze doré and porcelain hinged box, curved shape, 4½"l x 3¼" x 1⅔".

Ivory portrait miniature of lady artist signed Drea, hand-painted floral cartouche on bottom, rose pompadour.

$1,000.00 – 1,200.00.

Close-up of portrait.

Open view.

Jewelry box.

Sevres style, c. 1890s.

Hinged box, 4½"l x 3⅞" x 2⅛".

Gold with hand-painted flowers, white cartouche with gilt decoration.

$250.00 – 300.00.

Trinket box.

Sevres style, c. 1870 – 1890s, artist signed H. Boit.

Egg-shaped hinged box, 5"w.

Hand-painted courting scene on lid, rich cobalt ground with raised gilt (see mark 91).

$300.00 – 350.00.

Close-up of lid.

Trinket box.

Sevres style, c. 1900 – 1910.

Hinged box, 3½"l x 1½" x 1"h.

Hand-painted flowers on lid, light green border.

$100.00 – 125.00.

Casket box.

Sevres style, c. 1900 – 1920s.

Hinged box, 6¾" x 3½" x 2".

Pale pink with a garland of flowers, artist signed.

$150.00 – 200.00.

Trinket box.

Sevres style, c. 1900.

Hinged box, 2⅓" x 2" x 1½".

Magenta ground, cartouches of hand painted flowers.

$150.00 – 200.00.

Trinket box.

Paris in the Sevres style, unmarked, c. 1850 – 1890, artist signed Lucas.

Hinged and cylindrical in shape, 2½"d x 3".

Doré bronze lid and fittings with a miniature painting on ivory of a pretty young woman wearing a brimmed hat with flowers, bottom of the box beautifully hand painted with floral swags and gilt.

$350.00 – 400.00.

Close-up.

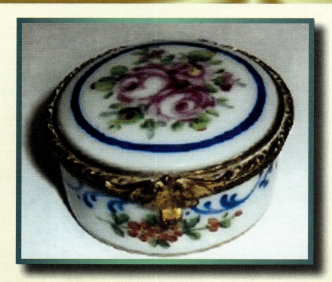

Patch box.

Sevres style, c. 1850 – 1860.

Hinged box.

Hand-painted roses on lid, dark blue band (see mark 89).

$100.00 – 125.00.

Figural bonbonniere.

French, unmarked, eighteenth century.

Figural hinged box, 2¼" x 1½" x 2".

Shepherd playing a flute with dog and two sheep beside him, polychromed flowers on bottom.

$400.00 – 450.00.

Back view.

Patch box.

French soft paste, unmarked, Eighteenth century.

Two part round box, 1¼"w x 1½"h.

Hand-painted flowers on lid with gold trim.

$75.00 – 95.00.

Etui.

French or German, unmarked.

Hinged, 3"l.

Transfer decoration.

$50.00 – 75.00.

Open view.

Figural snuff box.

French or German, c. 1830 – 1870.

Hinged box, 2¼"w x 2¾"h.

Rare figure of cat head.

$500.00 – 575.00.

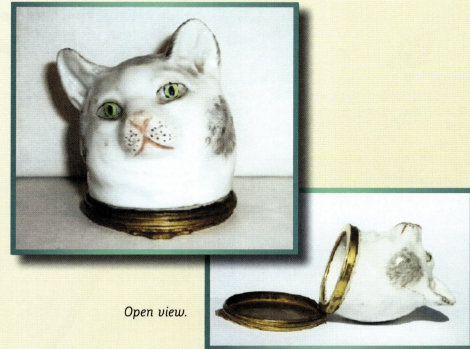

Open view.

German Boxes

There is a large variety of interesting German boxes available in all price ranges. Advanced collectors look for top quality, rare Meissen boxes. In the eighteenth century Meissen produced some of the best snuff boxes ever made. During the Victorian period an endless amount of interesting trinket boxes were exported to the United States. Novelty elfinware boxes were made in the early twentieth century and attract many collectors today.

MAKERS

MEISSEN

Meissen, the first European porcelain company, was founded in Meissen, Germany, in 1710 under the patronage of Augustus the Strong. Count Bruhl became the administrator of Meissen in 1737. During his directorship, Meissen produced large quantities of porcelain snuff boxes, many hand painted with exquisite scenes. Count Bruhl had an extensive wardrobe, and each outfit had a snuff box to go with it. When he died, over 700 snuff boxes were put up for sale.

Eighteenth century snuff boxes made by Meissen are rare today. Most of the early boxes had gold or silver mounts. They are valued at auction in the $2,000 – 6,000 price range. Figural boxes are especially popular. For example, a Meissen figural lemon box dating 1750 – 1760 with some repairs and with petal and leaf chips would sell for about $2,500.

A Meissen gold mounted cartouche-shaped snuff box modeled by J. Kaendler with a courting scene on the lid and camaieu harbor scene on the base with a pug dog on the lid in relief might sell for $10,000 – 15,000 at auction.

The eighteenth century snuff boxes were well decorated on the inside; in fact, the inside was the "show" side of the box. Many of the snuff boxes were given as royal gifts and might have a portrait of the king inside or a special surprise painting.

Meissen also made toilet sets in the eighteenth century. A toilet set decorated with Watteau scenes in copper green was a popular pattern for the ladies of the royal court.

Many toilet sets and snuff boxes were decorated with the same patterns as on Meissen's tableware. Popular patterns were chinoiseries, battle scenes, Watteau paintings, and strewn flowers. Today, a variety of late nineteenth century and twentieth century Meissen boxes can be found. Some might be hinged in a heart, oval, cartouche, or round shape. Two part dresser boxes in cobalt blue with flowers or allegorical scenes are popular as well as boxes in the Purple and Green Indian, Blue Onion, and Court Dragon patterns.

Meissen trinket box, Purple Indian pattern.

DRESDEN

Between 1850 and 1914 as many as 200 decorating studios evolved in and around Dresden, creating a Dresden style which was a mixture of Meissen and Vienna. Some of the decorators, especially Ambrosias Lamm made beautiful boxes to match or even outdo Meissen and Vienna. Popular decorating styles were simple paintings of lifelike flowers on a pure white background, Watteau courting scenes, and cherubs with burnished gilt.

FRANZISKA HIRSCH

Franziska Hirsch operated a porcelain studio on Struwestrasse 19 in Dresden from 1894 to 1930, decorating in the Meissen and Vienna styles. The company's early marks were variations of crossed lines or staffs and the initial "H" in overglaze blue. In 1896 Meissen successfully won a lawsuit against Hirsch's use of the two crossed staffs with the "H." A new mark of a stylized "H" with wings and Dresden were then used by Hirsch.

Hirsch used blanks by Meissen, Rosenthal, and MZ Austria and used the gold overglaze flower to hide the manufacturer's mark. The favorite decorative style used by Hirsch was Dresden flowers in bouquets or star garlands on a pristine white ground with gilt borders.

Many dresser boxes were produced with hand-painted flowers and gilt decoration. Hirsch decorated boxes in a variety of shapes, including egg, bellows, round, quatrefoil, square, and figural. An interesting two part floral decorated box in the shape of a turtle is valued at $350 – 450. Hirsch also decorated some special jeweled boxes with Tiffany luster glazes.

RICHARD KLEMM

Karl Richard Klemm had a decorating studio on Vorstadt Striesen in Dresden c. 1869 – 1949. Klemm was an outstanding artist in his own right and was known for painting in the Meissen and Vienna styles.

A number of trademarks were used by Richard Klemm. His studio was part of the cooperative using the crown Dresden mark in 1883. It also included Donath & Co., Oswald Lorenz, and Adolph Hamann. Apart from the group crown Dresden mark, Klemm also used a monogram mark consisting of a reversed R joined to a K under a crown with the word Dresden below.

Blanks commonly used were by Meissen, Rosenthal, KPM, Silesia Porcelain Factory, and Limoges. Klemm painted boxes with Watteau courting scenes alternating with florals. Popular colors used were apple green, black, pink, yellow, and blue.

Klemm produced some top quality work for important clients. An example is a round two part box with a portrait of Ruth holding a sheaf of wheat which is valued at $200 – 225.

AMBROSIUS LAMM

Ambrosius Lamm operated a porcelain painting studio and arts and antique shop from 1887 to 1949. It was located at Zinzendorfstrasse 28 in Dresden. He had approximately 25 employees by 1894 which grew to about 40 in 1907.

Lamm's studio is known for painting in the Meissen, Vienna, and Copenhagen style. He bought blanks from a number of manufacturing firms including Meissen, Rosenthal, Hutschenreuther, and Silesia.

At least three different marks were used by Lamm, including a pensive angel with Dresden and Saxony, L within a shield, and the most common mark, a painting of a lamb with Dresden underneath. He apparently attempted to use a crossed swords mark as well because Meissen took action against him in 1943.

The Lamm studio consistently produced work of outstanding quality. Lamm decorated boxes that rivaled the quality of Royal Vienna and Sevres. Many examples can be found with cherubs holding fruit and flowers and playing musical instruments. They were often portrayed amidst fluffy clouds.

Lamm produced a series of small boxes with hand-painted raised gold silhouettes of a man and woman dancing in different ground colors. He also made small round boxes with gold interiors and hand-painted courting scene medallions framed by gold beads. A variety of ground colors were used, and these boxes are valued at

$150 – 175. The borders on Lamm's boxes were often a rich cobalt blue. Lamm was a master of gilding and heavy paste decoration.

Dresden Lamm box with courting scene on apple green ground.

CARL THIEME

Carl Thieme was possibly one of the best copycats of Meissen porcelain. He started a china decorating studio in Potschappel, Germany, in 1867. The town is located in eastern Germany in the state of Saxony between the foothills of the Erzgebirge Mountains and ten miles from Dresden. In 1921 the town was combined with the villages of Deuben and Doehlen to form the city of Freital. The company is still in business today.

Thieme's studio decorated porcelain whiteware it bought from the C. G. Schierholz factory in Plaue, Saxony, in the Meissen and Vienna styles. On October 2, 1872, the company began producing its own porcelain and was named Saxon Porcelain Manufactory Dresden. One of the frequently used marks from 1888 to 1901 was crossed lines with a T in underglaze or overglaze blue or black.

Carl Thieme made a variety of decorative boxes in square, rectangular, heart, and round shapes, primarily with hand-painted floral decoration. He copied the allover applied flowers boxes made by Meissen, and these are popular with collectors.

RICHARD WEHSNER

Richard Wehsner ran a porcelain studio at Zinzendorfstrasse 16 in Dresden from 1895 to 1956. The company produced finely painted Meissen type decoration for export. Wehsner decorated boxes for dresser and desk sets. The flower painting was outstanding. It decorated some top quality portrait boxes as well, ranging in price from $500 to $600.

HELENA WOLFSOHN

The earliest Dresden studio to copy Meissen's designs was Helena Wolfsohn which began operation in 1843. During the period 1875 – 1915 there were 30 painters working at the studio.

Helena Wolfsohn used various forms of A R in script from 1843 to 1883. In 1879 Meissen took Wolfsohn to court regarding the use of the A R mark. Wolfsohn won, and Meissen appealed it. It was over-turned in 1881. At this time the firm adopted a mark using a crown with the letter D underneath. Wolfsohn also used the word Dresden, surmounted by a crown. The gold overglaze flower mark was used from 1880 to 1945 to cover the manufacturer's mark.

Wolfsohn purchased white china blanks from the Meissen factory and had them decorated by her own staff of painters and gilders. The workshop of Helena Wolfsohn was one of the most prolific decorating studios in Dresden. Wolfsohn produced boxes with floral decoration and courting scenes. She decorated a number of top quality dresser boxes with allegorical and battle scene decorations in the Meissen and Vienna styles. They range in price from $400 to $500.

Battle scene. Postcard, Raphael Tuck & Sons, "Oilette," British Battles, Series I, #9134.

HEUBACH BROTHERS

Some of the most valuable bisque (unglazed porcelain) boxes were made by the Heubach Brothers, a company located in Lichte, Thuringia, operating from 1822 to the present. A common Heubach mark is a circular rising sun device containing an H over C. Although best known for their bisque dolls and figures, the company also made some wonderful bisque boxes.

One rare Heubach bisque box has a pale yellow basketweave design.

Rare Heubach bisque box, c. 1890 – 1920s.

Four adorable busts of babies look out of the box. Another has a figure of a baby with a beach ball sitting on a pink tassel pillow. These boxes are valued from $1,500 – 2,000.

KPM

Frederick the Great, whose passion was white gold, gave KPM (Kings Porcelain Manufactory) its name and trademark, the royal blue scepter in 1763. It is located in Berlin, Germany, and is one of the top porcelain companies in the world. It is still in operation today.

KPM produced some snuff boxes in the eighteenth century, but they are quite rare and in private collections. An example is a cylindrical box dating c. 1770 – 1775 with gold mounts and well painted mythological scenes on the lid and on the sides.

KPM is especially known for its realistic flower and fruit painting, and some lovely dresser boxes with a molded flower bud finial can be found today.

ROYAL BAYREUTH

The Royal Bayreuth company has a long history, beginning in 1794. It operated under the name Porcelain Factory Tettau from 1902 until 1957. In 1957, the company adopted the name, Royally Privileged Porcelain Factory Tettau GMBH, which it still uses today. Today the firm produces dinnerware and limited edition collectibles.

Royal Bayreuth made a variety of boxes that are eagerly collected. Figurals include tomatoes, grapes, lemons, poppies, lobsters, and the popular Devil and Cards. It also made boxes in its

Royal Bayreuth Rose Tapestry dresser box, c. 1902 – 1920.

popular tapestry patterns. Tapestry boxes were made by wrapping the porcelain in a coarse cloth and then firing it. The cloth burned away leaving a rough ground that felt like woven cloth. The piece was then glazed. Decoration was added over the glaze. Royal Bayreuth used flowers, scenes, birds, and portrait transfers as decoration. Rose Tapestry is the most popular and a box having this decoration would be valued in the $300 range.

SCHAFER & VATER

This partnership was established in Rudolstadt, Thuringia, by Gustav Schafer & Gunther Vater in 1890. In 1972 the East German government took possession of the building and destroyed all records and molds. Bisque figural trinket boxes and novelty pieces are very popular with collectors.

VON SCHIERHOLZ

C. G. Schierholz & Sons was founded in Plaue, Thuringia, in 1817. After the family was knighted, the name was changed in 1900 to von Schierholz Porcelain Manufactory. The company made some interesting trinket and potpourri boxes with applied figures of birds and Cupids on the lids. The boxes usually have hand-painted flowers and gilt in the Dresden style.

SITZENDORF

The Voight family established this porcelain manufactory in 1840 in Sitzendorf, Germany. Porcelain was made in the Dresden style. Sitzendorf porcelain was marked with two parallel lines crossed by a third line. Twentieth century Sitzendorf is marked with the original crossed lines, superimposed on a crown and letter S.

The company produced a number of lovely dresser boxes. Many were decorated with applied pink and yellow flowers. Cupids were a popular addition to many of Sitzendorf's decorative wares, including boxes.

VOLKSTEDT

Volkstedt has a long and complicated history, and there are at least six factories that carried the name. The company made some excellent quality snuff boxes in the eighteenth century. Most were mounted in silver gilt, and were decorated with hunting or landscape scenes. Portrait boxes were also produced. During the nineteenth century boxes were made in a variety of shapes, most with hand-painted flowers or courting scenes.

CHARMING MOSS COVERED ELFINWARE BOXES

A growing number of collectors have begun to appreciate the charm of elfinware. These miniature Dresden-like porcelain novelties were made in Germany between World War I and II and were sold in gift shops and department stores.

Webster's Dictionary defines "elfin" as small and charming, and most pieces of elfinware are just that — ranging in size from one inch to five inches. There are a few exceptions. A full-size teapot and coffee pot have been discovered, as well as a 12 inch high dresser lamp.

Many pieces of elfinware are unmarked. Others have "Germany" or "Made in Germany" stamped in black or dark red. A few have been found with a gift shop's name. One maker's mark has been found on a piano box of beautiful quality. The manufacturer, the Orben, Knabe and Company, was located in Geschwenda, Thuringia, Germany, and made decorative porcelains, souvenir, and gift articles from 1910 to 1939. Elfinware was probably made by several other porcelain companies in and around the Thuringian region of East Germany, where the application of flowers to china became an art form renown the world over.

Elfinware items have a fairly coarse porcelain body. Characteristic of many German porcelains, the base is usually bisque in order to allow the object to grip a surface better. Some pieces have a pearlized lustrous finish, usually in blue, light green, or orange. Many pieces are decorated with a dark reddish brown trim.

Most pieces of elfinware are decorated in the style of Meissen or Dresden with applied flowers. Boxes often have floral decals to enhance the inside or sides. Most items have a large applied white rose with a pink center. The pieces are further encrusted with many applied forget-me-nots. One row of deep blue flowers with yellow centers usually lines the top of the piece. Pink, white, and aqua forget-me-nots and daisies are also in abundance, as well as violets. The name "forget–me–not" comes from an old German legend that tells of a knight who drowned while swimming to get some of the blue flowers for his sweetheart. His last words to her were, "Forget-me-not."

Box with forget-me-nots, violets.
German postcard GR Co. #107.

The most unique and charming characteristic is the moss or "spinach" that is encrusted on many pieces. This decoration is similar to a technique used by Bernard Palissy, the early French potter (1510 – 1590). Palissy's ware was encrusted with organic decoration and animals. The elfinware "moss" is a hand-whipped coarse, grouty bisque in two shades of green that was probably applied to the piece by a tube-similar to today's cake decorating techniques. Moss encrusted pieces are avidly hunted by collectors today, and prices are more than double the pieces without moss.

A variety of elfinware boxes were created to delight collectors. Boxes with animals and birds in relief on the lid are the rarest and most

valuable pieces, and prices range from $200 to $400+. They were made in a variety of shapes, such as oval, round, rectangular, and heart shaped. Boxes in the shape of a grand piano are quite popular and were made in all sizes,

Elfinware box in the form of piano.

WORDS FROM AN ELFINWARE COLLECTOR

"It started with a small figural piece, but once I found a beautiful moss covered heart-shaped box, I fell in love with the covered boxes," explains Judy Brim, who along with her husband, Larry and their family, live in Prior, Oklahoma. Brim has been collecting elfinware for about 18 years. We greatly appreciate her sharing many photographs from her wonderful collection.

Brim found her first elfinware box at a flea market. She laments, "One used to find a lot of elfinware in flea markets, antique shows, and malls but with so many collectors now and with the internet opening up the world, it is becoming harder to find rare pieces. When I began collecting, a lot of dealers or individuals did not know what elfinware was. With the internet came knowledge, so that is not the case now."

Brim says she finds the boxes interesting because there are so many differently shaped ones. One of her very favorites is in the shape of an airplane. She tells us she likes the boxes with animals on the lids and musical powder boxes. One of her favorites is a footed marble powder box with brass ormolu fittings.

"Boxes with colorful fruit applied on the top really appeal to me. I recently found a very old one that was oval shaped and has a hinged lid with part of the inner lining still intact," Brim explains.

Brim tells us she enjoys searching for boxes she doesn't now own as one never knows what might show up or where. "This collecting has been a fun experience in my life, and I have a sister, mom, and two daughters that are into collecting elfinware now. It has become a family affair."

VICTORIAN TRINKET BOXES

"The charm of the Victorian trinket box lies in the wide variety of subjects and decoration adorning the covers." (*Victorian Trinket Boxes* by Janice and Richard Vogel)

During the Victorian era (1837 – 1901), it was popular for shelves, tables, and mantels to be covered with knick knacks. Trinket boxes were made in porcelain, bisque, and earthenware in all shapes and sizes and were displayed proudly in middle class homes.

German bisque trinket box, c. 1890 – 1920.

Most of the trinket books collected today were made in Germany. Conta & Boehme, 1790 – 1937, was a leading manufacturer of trinket boxes exported in large quantities to Great Britain and the United States. The mark is usually an impressed shield containing a raised arm holding a dagger.

Conta & Boehme made a variety of collectible trinket boxes, including inkwell boxes; miniature boxes from one to three inches; boxes with children, animals, fruit, and flowers in relief on the lids; and mirrored dresser boxes. A rattle-holding infant wrapped in bunting with a blanket cover was a popular novelty box made by Conta & Boehme. It comes in six sizes and is usually unmarked. It is valued at $175 – 225. The company made a similar box with a figure of a cat lying down covered with a blanket.

Some of the most popular trinket boxes were those with animals on the lid. Many were inspired from eighteenth century snuff boxes. A black box with a bisque kitten with a blue bow perched on the lid with another kitten's head protruding from the bottom part of the box is highly collectible and valued at $400 – $500.

Fairings, often made in the form of cosmetic or trinket boxes were also popular items made by Conta & Boehme and well as other German companies. From 1850 to 1918 they were exported to England to be used as prizes at fairs. They are small chinaware figural groups and boxes that portray amusing, and sometime risqué, scenes of courting couples, marital woes, and parenthood. They often have mottos or humerous expressions, such as, "When a man marries, his troubles begin."

Interesting social documents of the time, fairings are eagerly collected. Some were used as match holders and strikers. A hollow container is worked into the design, and part of the base is roughened to provide a striking surface.

Many people confuse the fairings as Staffordshire, but they were not made in England. After World War I German wares were not favored in the United States, and products from England were very popular. Some dishonest dealers falsely attributed the fairing boxes as being made in England in order to generate more sales.

Fairings have been reproduced by several Japanese companies. The Original Arnart Creations is one of the largest reproducers of porcelains in Japan, and it reproduced many Conta & Boehme items. Its mark was a four-feathered crossed arrow mark.

German fairing box figure of cat, probably made by Conta & Boehme.

Fairing box with kitten, Germany.

Matchbox.

Conta & Boehme, c. 1890 – 1920s.

Two part box shaped like dog house, striking surface on the side of the house.

Dog coming from front of house looking up at white cat on roof.

$300.00 – 350.00.

Front view.

Back view.

Dresser box.

Dresden, Donath & Co., c. 1890s.

Round two part box, 5¼".

Yellow fish scale border, hand-painted flowers on side and all over on inside, courting scene on lid (see mark 14).

$275.00 – 300.00.

Close-up.

Figural box.

Dresden, Hirsch, F., c. 1893 – 1920.

Two part figural box in form of turtle, 7½"l x 4¾"h.

Hand-painted flowers and gilt (see mark 16).

$350.00 – 450.00.

Open view.

Powder box.

Dresden, Hirsch, F., c. 1890s.

Two part box, 3½"w x 2"h.

Art Nouveau style decoration, purple luster with gilt grape leaves and pearl jeweling, eight petal gold flowers with gold beads and turquoise jewels on lid (see mark 15).

$300.00 – 350.00.

Trinket box.

Dresden, Hirsch, Franziska, c. 1901 – 1930.

Egg-shaped two part box.

Hand-painted garlands and vases of flowers, gilt crosshatching.

$175.00 – 200.00.

German Boxes

Two pin boxes.

Dresden, Hirsch, Franziska, c. 1901 – 1930.

Small boxes with lids.

Hand-painted flowers and gilt.

$95.00 – 125.00 each.

Figural box.

Dresden, Hirsch, Franziska, c. 1900 – 1920.

Two part bellows shaped box, 7¾"l x 2⅛"h.

Hand-painted flowers and gilt.

$200.00 – 225.00.

Open view.

Trinket box.

Dresden, Hutschenreuther, c. 1900 – 1920.

Two part quatrefoil shaped box, 2⅓" x 1¾".

Cobalt blue with raised gold flowers (see mark 17).

$75.00 – 95.00.

Powder box.

Dresden, Hutschenreuther,
c. 1918 – 1945.

Round two part box, 3" x 2¼"h.

All gold with green hand-painted
courting scenes on lid in Meissen
style (see mark 18).

$150.00 – 175.00.

Close-up.

Portrait box.

Dresden, Klemm, R., c. 1900 – 1920s.

Round two part box, 2¼" x 1¼".

Portrait of Ruth holding a
sheaf of wheat (see mark 19).

$200.00 – 225.00.

Close-up.

Two trinket boxes.

Dresden, Klemm, Richard, c. 1891 – 1914.

(Left) Square box on four gold curved feet. (Right) Rectangular fluted box; delicate floral and gilt painting.

$150.00 – 175.00 each.

Dresser box.

Dresden, Koch, Wilhelm, c. 1928 – 1949.

Scalloped two-part box, 3½"w x 5"l x 1¾"h.

Hand-painted courting scene alternating with flowers on yellow ground (see mark 20).

$300.00 – 400.00.

Dresser box.

Dresden, Lamm, Ambrosius, c. 1885 – 1890s.

Round hinged box, 3½".

Hand-painted courting scene on lid, cobalt blue ground with gilt decoration, hand-painted flowers inside (see mark 21).

$300.00 – 375.00.

Another view.

Rouge box.

Dresden, Lamm, Ambrosius, c. 1890s.

Two part round box, gold interior, 2½".

Hand-painted raised gold silhouettes of man and woman dancing, cobalt ground (see mark 22).

$175.00 – 225.00.

Rouge box.

Dresden, Lamm, Ambrosius, c. 1890s.

Two part round box, 2½".

Hand-painted flowers inside and out, gilt rim.

$125.00 – 150.00.

Trinket box.

Dresden, Lamm, Ambrosius, c. 1931 – 1945.

Octagonal two part box; hand-painted basket of flowers motif, raised gold.

$150.00 – 175.00.

Rouge box.

Dresden, Lamm, Ambrosius, c. 1890s.

Two part round box,
gold interior, 2¼".

Dark red ground,
hand-painted courting scene
medallions framed by gold beads.

$150.00 – 175.00.

Close-up of lid.

Same box in dark green.

Same box
in blue.

Open view.

Same box in apple green.

Dresser box.

Dresden, Thieme, Carl,
c. 1920 – 1930s.

Two part box, 4"w x 3¼"h.

Allover applied flowers
(see mark 23).

$200.00 – 250.00.

Another view.

Trinket box.

Dresden, Thieme, Carl,
c. 1920 – 1930s.

Two part box, 3⅓"l x 2⅓"w x 1½"h.

Hand-painted flowers
inside and out, gilt decoration.

$125.00 – 150.00.

Close-up of lid.

Trinket box.

Dresden, Thieme, Carl,
c. 1901 – present.

Two part box with molded scrolls,
3¾"w x 3½"h.

Hand-painted flowers.

$75.00 – 100.00.

Trinket box.

Dresden, Thieme, Carl,
c. 1901 – 1930s.

Square hinged box, 4".

Hand-painted flowers.

$125.00 – 150.00.

Trinket box.

Dresden, Thieme, Carl,
c. 1950 – 1970s.

Heart-shaped two part
box with leaf finial.

Vivid hand-painted
flowers and gilt trim on rims.

$100.00 – 125.00.

Trinket box.

Dresden, Thieme, Carl,
c. 1901 – 1920s.

Hinged rectangular box.

Hand-painted harbor scene on
lid, strewn flowers inside.

$150.00 – 175.00.

Trinket box.

Dresden, Thieme, Carl, c. 1901 – 1930s.

Two part heart-shaped box, 2¼" x 1¾".

Light peach ground, applied
flowers all over lid and bottom.

$150.00 – 200.00.

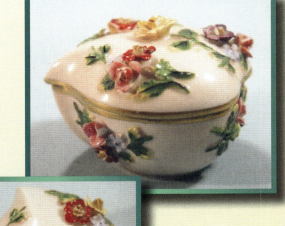

Close-up.

Pair dresser boxes.

Dresden, Wehsner, Richard,
c. 1895 – 1918.

Two part boxes with applied rose finial
on lids.

Excellent flower painting, gilt rims.

$150.00 – 175.00 each.

Potpourri box.

Dresden, Thieme, Carl, c. 1920s.

Two part reticulated box, 2¾".

Gold decoration and applied flowers.

$175.00 – 200.00.

Another view.

Close-up.

Portrait box.

Dresden, Wehsner, Richard, c. 1890s.

Two part box.

Hand-painted top quality portrait of beautiful woman with white hat, Royal Vienna style decoration (see mark 24).

$500.00 – 600.00.

Close-up of gilding.

Close-up of portrait.

Stamp box.

Dresden, Wehsner, Richard, c. 1890s.

Two part box with ruffled foot, three slanted compartments for stamps, 3¾" x 1¾" x 1¼".

Hand-painted blue flowers with molded gold swirls.

$200.00 – 225.00.

Another view.

Dresser box.

Dresden, Wolfsohn, H., c. 1890s.

Two part round box, 3¾".

Allegorical painting of a courting scene on lid, cobalt ground with gilt decoration.

$400.00 – 450.00.

Close-up of lid.

Dresser box.

Dresden, Wolfsohn, H., c. 1890s.

Round hinged box.

Hand-painted battle scene on lid, cobalt and gilt (see mark 26).

$450.00 – 500.00.

Close-up of battle scene.

Open view.

Dresser box.

Dresden, Wolfsohn, H., c. 1900 – 1920.

Round two part box.

Hand-painted flowers with gilt, courting scene on lid.

$125.00 – 175.00.

Dresser box.

Dresden, Helena Wolfsohn,
c. 1886 – 1891.

Scalloped round two part box,
4" x 1½"h.

Hand-painted courting scene on
lid, garlands of flowers on border
(see mark 25).

$200.00 – 225.00.

Close-up.

Large dresser box.

Dresden, Helena Wolfsohn, c. 1886 – 1891.

Square box, 7⅓"w x 1¾"h.

Hand-painted courting scene lid with floral cartouches, gilt decoration.

$500.00 – 600.00.

Close-up.

View of lid.

Trinket box.

Dresden, unknown decorator, c. 1870.

Unusual shaped hinged box, 3½" x 2".

Hand-painted flowers inside and out, cobalt border with gilt.

$250.00 – 275.00.

Open view.

Figural box.

Elfinware, c. 1910 – 1930s.

Two part box in form of airplane, 2½"w x 3¾"l x 1½"h.

Applied flowers and forget-me-nots, moss encrusted.

$300.00 – 400.00.

Figural box.

Elfinware, c. 1910 – 1930s.

Two part box with figure of hen on lid.

White basketweave on bottom, lid with moss and forget-me-nots.

$200.00 – 250.00.

Trinket box.

Elfinware, Orben, Knabe & Co., c. 1910 – 1930s.

Two part box with four scrolled feet, 5¼" x 3½".

Nice quality with applied forget-me-nots and flowers, moss encrusted (see mark 27).

$250.00 – 300.00.

Figural box.

Elfinware, Orben, Knabe & Co., c. 1910 – 1930s.

Grand piano box, 4½" x 3¼"h.

Applied forget-me-nots and flowers, moss encrusted.

$200.00 – 250.00.

Another view.

Trinket box.

Elfinware, c. 1910 – 1930s.

Round two part box.

Figure of dog in center of lid, applied forget-me-nots and flowers, moss encrusted.

$150.00 – 175.00.

Dresser box.

Elfinware, c. 1910 – 1930s.

Round two part box.

Applied forget-me-nots and flowers, moss encrusted.

$60.00 – 75.00.

Flower holder box.

Elfinware, c. 1910 – 1930s.

Round two part box, reticulated lid.

Applied forget-me-nots and flowers, moss encrusted.

$100.00 – 125.00.

Trinket box.

Elfinware, c. 1910 – 1930s.

Two part rectangular box.

Applied flowers on lid.

$45.00 – 60.00.

Trinket box.

Elfinware, c. 1910 – 1930s.

Two part rectangular box.

Applied forget-me-nots and flowers, moss encrusted.

$75.00 – 100.00.

Trinket box.

Elfinware, c. 1910 – 1930s.

Two part oval box.

Applied forget-me-nots and flowers, moss encrusted.

$75.00 – 100.00.

Figural box.

Elfinware, c. 1910 – 1930s.

Small two part box in form of piano, 2½"w x 1¾".

Applied flowers with moss on lid and sides.

$90.00 – 125.00.

Open view.

Figural box.

Elfinware, c. 1910 – 1930s.

Two part box in form of piano, 3"l x 2"w x 1½"h.

Hand-painted fruit in relief on lid, floral transfer on side.

$175.00 – 200.00.

Trinket box.

Elfinware, c. 1910 – 1930s.

Two part box with figure of bird on lid, 3¼"w x 4½"h.

Applied pink roses, forget-me-nots.

$75.00 – 100.00.

Trinket box.

Elfinware, c. 1910 – 1930s.

Two part box with figure of bird on lid, 3¼"w x 4½"h.

Applied white roses on orange luster.

$75.00 – 100.00.

Trinket box.

Elfinware, c. 1910 – 1930s.

Two part box, 4½"w x 2½"h.

Cream ground, lid covered with applied flowers and blue and violet forget-me-nots.

$45.00 – 60.00.

Trinket box.

Elfinware, c. 1910 – 1930s.

Rare heart–shaped two part box,
4½"l x 4¼"w x 2¼"h.

Applied forget-me-nots and
flowers, moss encrusted.

$125.00 – 150.00.

Trinket box.

Elfinware, c. 1910 – 1930s.

Two part box, white basketweave
design on bottom.

Applied forget-me-nots and flowers,
moss encrusted.

$60.00 – 75.00.

Dresser box.

Elfinware, c. 1910 – 1930s.

Marble box with brass fittings
and round feet, 4½"d x 3¼"h.

Plaque on lid with applied
forget-me-nots and flowers.

$125.00 – 150.00.

Another view.

Jewelry music box.

Elfinware, c. 1910 – 1930s.

Brass reticulated box with ornate feet, mirror in lid, glass insert in bottom, 3½"d x 5"h.

Porcelain plaque insert in lid with applied flowers and forget-me-nots.

$200.00 – 250.00.

Close-up.

Trinket box.

Elfinware, c. 1910 – 1930s.

Round two part box, 2"d x 2"h.

White ground, applied forget-me-nots and flowers, moss encrusted, figure of cat in center of lid.

$125.00 – 150.00.

German Boxes

Trinket box or basket.

Elfinware, c. 1910 – 1930s.

Two part basketweave style box with handle, 6"l x 4"w x 5½"h.

Applied forget-me-nots and flowers, moss encrusted.

$50.00 – 75.00.

Open view.

Trinket box.

Elfinware, c. 1910 – 1930s.

Unusual shaped two part box, 5¼"l x 3½"w x 3"h.

White basketweave ground; applied forget-me-nots and flowers, moss encrusted on lid.

$100.00 – 125.00.

Figural box.

Elfinware, c. 1910 – 1930s.

Two part box in shape of piano, 6¼"l x 4½"w x 5"h.

Applied forget-me-nots and flowers, moss encrusted.

$175.00 – 200.00.

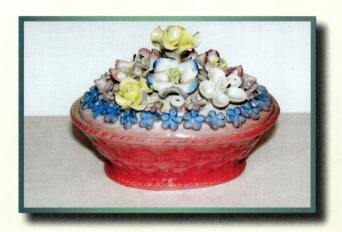

Trinket box.

Elfinware, c. 1910 – 1930s.

Two part box, 4"l x 3"w x 3"h.

Rose ground, applied forget-me-nots and flowers on lid.

$75.00 – 95.00.

Trinket box.

Elfinware, c. 1910 – 1930s.

Two part box.

Applied forget-me-nots and flowers moss encrusted.

$100.00 – 125.00.

Open view.

Figural box.

Heubach, c. 1890 – 1920s.

Bisque two part box.

Figure of cute puppy dog with lace outfit (see mark 34).

$700.00 – 900.00.

Figural box.

Heubach, c. 1890 – 1920s.

Bisque two part box, 8"l x 5"w x 6½"h.

Pale yellow basketweave design, four adorable busts of babies looking out of box.

$1,500.00 – 1,600.00.

Close-up.

Figural box.

Heubach, c. 1890 – 1920s.

Rare box, 5¼" x 5¾"h.

Figure of adorable baby with beach ball sitting on pink tassel pillow.

$2,000.00+.

Dresser box.

KPM, c. 1890s.

Round two part box, 3½" x 3¾"h.

White ground, hand-painted flowers and gilt, gold and white flower bud finial (see mark 36).

$150.00 – 200.00.

Portrait box.

Hutschenreuther porcelain plaque,
c. 1910 – 1920.

Hinged bronze doré box with applied leafy
decoration, 2¼" x 2½".

Lid has painting on porcelain portrait of a
beautiful Asti lady.

$600.00 – 650.00.

Another view.

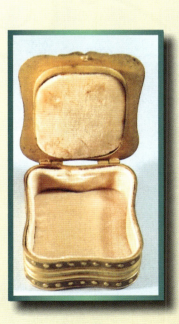

Open view.

Dresser box.

KPM Berlin, c. 1920s.

Round two part box,
flower bud finial.

Molded flowers, gilt decoration on
border (see mark 35).

$100.00 – 125.00.

Trinket box.

Meissen, c. 1824 – 1850.

Two part box, handle with entwined stem, 3" x 2¼".

Covered with applied flowers.

$450.00 – 500.00.

Open view.

Trinket box.

Meissen, c. 1850 – 1924.

Heart-shaped hinged box, 2¾".

Yellow ground, white and gold cherry blossoms in relief (see mark 59).

$300.00 – 350.00.

Another view.

Dresser box.

Meissen, c. 1950 – 1970.

Round two part box, 3"w x 1¾"h.

Cobalt blue ground, hand-painted flowers framed by gold decoration on lid.

$250.00 – 300.00.

Open view.

Snuff box.

Meissen, c. 1850 – 1900.

Hinged box, 3" x 2¼".

Exquisite hand-painted allegorical scene on lid, floral cartouches on sides, hand-painted floral bouquets on bottom and inside, turquoise blue ground with raised gold and beads.

$1,000.00 – 1,200.00.

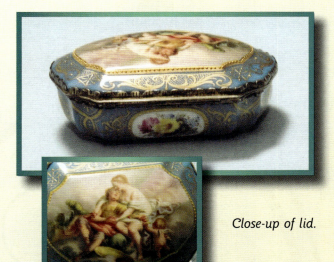

Close-up of lid.

Open view.

Painting on the bottom of the box.

Dresser box.

Meissen, c. 1850 – 1900.

Two part box, 3½" x 4"h.

White ground covered all over with applied flowers, pink rose in center of lid.

$600.00 – 700.00.

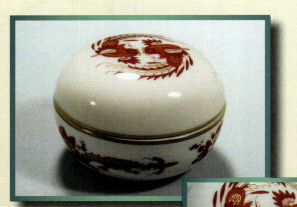

Dresser box.

Meissen, c. 1953 – 1957.

Two part box, 3½" x 2½".

Red Court Dragon pattern (see mark 60).

$250.00 – 300.00.

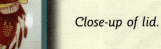

Close-up of lid.

Dresser box.

Meissen, c. 1950s.

Two part box, 3¾"w x 2¼"h.

Rich cobalt blue ground with hand-painted flowers on lid framed by gold decoration.

$300.00 – 350.00.

Close-up.

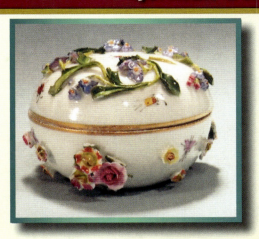

Dresser box.

Meissen, c. 1850 – 1924.

Two part box, 2¾".

Allover applied flowers with hand-painted bugs and butterflies.

$400.00 – 450.00.

Trinket box.

Meissen, c. 1970s.

Two part box, 3¾"l x 2⅔"w x 1½"h.

Hand-painted Purple Indian pattern.

$200.00 – 250.00.

Dresser box.

Meissen, c. 1970s.

Two part box, 2¾".

Green Indian pattern, gilt.

$175.00 – 200.00.

Open view.

German Boxes

Dresser box.

Meissen, c. 1930s.

Two part round shallow box.

Hand-painted rose decoration, gilt trim.

$75.00 – 100.00.

Dresser box.

Meissen, c. 1950s.

Two part round box, 3½"w x 2"h.

Red and gold Court Dragon pattern.

$250.00 – 275.00.

Dresser box.

Meissen, c. 1950s.

Two part round box, 3" x 1¾".

Green Ming Dragon pattern.

$275.00 – 300.00.

Close-up.

Dresser box.

Meissen, c. 1950s.

Two part box, 3¾" x 2⅔" x 1½".

Hand-painted green flowers and gilt.

$200.00 – 250.00.

Dresser box.

Meissen, c. 1850 – 1924.

Round hinged box with sterling silver mounts, 6¼"d x 3½"h.

Hand-painted flowers and insects on lid and the sides.

$500.00 – 600.00.

Close-up of lid.

Dresser box.

Nymphenburg, c. 1920 – 1930.

Two part swirled box, 4¾"d x 3"h.

Hand-painted flowers, gilt trim (see mark 61).

$125.00 – 150.00.

Close-up.

German Boxes

Trinket box.

Royal Bayreuth, c. 1902 – 1920.

Two part tapestry box, 4"l x 2"w x 1½"h.

Hand-painted peacock in scenic setting, water lilies on bottom (see mark 80).

$250.00 – 300.00.

Another view.

Dresser box.

Royal Bayreuth, c. 1902 – 1920.

Two part box.

Rose Tapestry pattern.

$275.00 – 325.00.

Trinket box.

Von Schierholz, c. 1907 – 1930s.

Two part round box.

Applied figure of bird surrounded by applied roses on lid; hand-painted roses (see mark 106).

$200.00 – 250.00.

Potpourri box.

Von Schierholz, c. 1930s.

Two part reticulated figural box, three curved feet, 4".

Cupid in relief with applied flowers.

$100.00 – 125.00.

Trinket box.

Von Schierholz, c. 1907 – 1930s.

Two part box, 4"l x 3½"w x 2¾"h.

Lid with applied bird figure, roses, and forget-me-nots.

$100.00 – 125.00.

Dresser box.

Von Schierholz, c. 1907 – 1930s.

Round two part box with slightly domed lid, 3"l x 2½"w x 2¼"h.

White with hand-painted blue forget-me-nots, applied roses and forget-me-nots covering lid.

$75.00 – 100.00.

Trinket box.

Schafer & Vater, c. 1920s.

Round two part egg-shaped box,
4¼"l x 3¼"w x 3½"h.

Yellow white ground, applied roses.

$75.00 – 95.00.

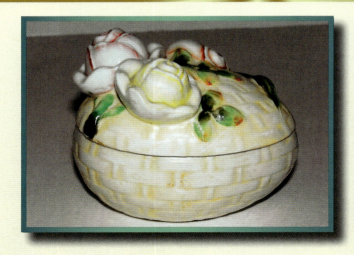

Trinket box.

Sitzendorf, c. 1900 – 1910.

Two part box.

Adorable figure of two babies on lid, applied
flowers (see mark 100).

$200.00 – 250.00.

Dresser box.

Teichert Co., Meissen, c. 1864 – 1900.

Two part box, 3½"w x 2¼"h.

Elaborate raised gold and jeweled decoration in
Vienna style, lid has square cartouche on lid
with courting scenes framed by raised gold (see mark 101).

$400.00 – 450.00.

Close-up.

Portrait box.

Volkstedt, c. 1787 – 1800.

Oval hinged box.

Hand-painted portrait of pretty woman on lid, magenta ground with gilt floral decoration (see mark 104).

$200.00 – 250.00.

Close-up.

Trinket box.

Volkstedt, c. 1870s.

Heart–shaped hinged box, 2¼".

Hand-painted flowers and gilt on lid and sides (see mark 105).

$200.00 – 225.00.

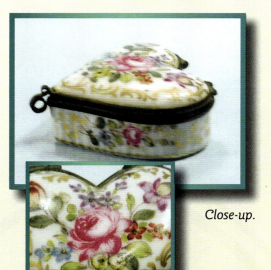

Close-up.

Close-up.

Trinket box.

Volkstedt, c. 1890s.

Hinged box, 2½" x 2", brass fleur-de-lis clasp.

Hand-painted flowers, gilt.

$175.00 – 200.00.

Open view.

Rouge box.

German, c. 1920s, unmarked.

Hinged, round, 1¾" x 1¼".

Transfer of Kaufmann allegorical painting.

$60.00 – 75.00.

Figural box.

Germany, imported by Borgfeldt & Sons, c. 1920 – 1930s.

Two part box, 4⅔"l x 3⅛" x 4".

Applied nude figure of a flapper girl reclining on a wavy plateau, Art Deco style (see mark 5).

$250.00 – 275.00.

Close-up of flapper girl.

Another view.

Figural box.

Germany, unmarked, c. 1890 – 1900.

Two part box with gray striped cat inside.

$150.00 – 175.00.

Open view.

Trinket box.

German, c. 1910 – 1930s.

Two part box with applied fruit, pearlized blue basketweave ground.

$100.00 – 125.00.

Trinket box.

German, c. 1910 – 1930s.

Two part round box, 3" x 2¼"h.

Blue luster, applied fruit on lid.

$75.00 – 100.00.

Trinket box.

German, c. 1910 – 1930s.

Two part oval box, 3¼" x 2" x 2¾"h.

White with applied fruit on lid.

$60.00 – 95.00.

Dresser box.

German, c. 1910 – 1930s.

Oval shaped brass box with etched grapes and leaf design, original cloth lining, 4"l x 3¼"w x 2½"h.

Porcelain plaque on lid with applied fruit.

$150.00 – 175.00.

Another view.

Open view.

Trinket box.

German, c. 1910 – 1930s.

Basketweave box, 2" x 1½" x 2¼"h.

Shades of brown, handle on lid with applied fruit.

$60.00 – 75.00.

Dresser box.

German, c. 1910 – 1930s.

Round two part white box with brass fittings, 6"d x 3½"h.

Applied fruit on lid, floral transfers inside box.

$150.00 – 175.00.

Open view.

Fairing box.

German, c. 1900 – 1920.

Two part box, 2¼"l x 2"w x 2¾"h.

Applied lily pad flowers and a cat and frog on lid.

$100.00 – 125.00.

Dresser box.

German, c. 1910 – 1930s.

Round two part box, 4"w x 2½"h.

Bright red ground, applied fruit on lid.

$100.00 – 125.00.

Open view.

Dresser box.

Bavarian, c. 1920 – 1930s.

Two part box, 5"l x 3¼"w x 1½"h.

Hand-painted roses, gilt trim, wear to gold on edge of rim (see mark 3).

$50.00 – 75.00.

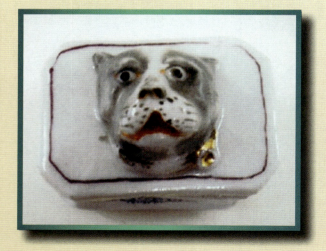

Figural box.

German, c. 1910 – 1930s.

Two part box, 2"w x 1⅛"h.

Figure of bulldog on lid.

$100.00 – 125.00.

Dresser box.

German, c. 1900 – 1930.

Round two part hinged box, 3½"w x 2½"h.

Figure of cat on lid, hand-painted flowers in relief.

$200.00 – 250.00.

Close-up.

Fairing box.

German, c. 1900.

Two part long box,
6½"l x 2½"w x 2½"h.

Figure of cat lying down covered with blanket, red floral decoration, yellow bows.

$200.00 – 250.00.

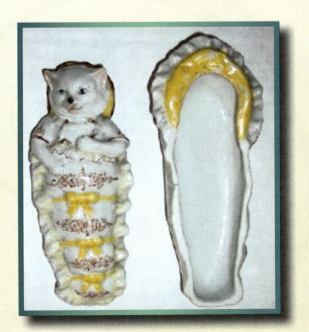

Open view.

Open view.

Fairing box.

German, c. 1900.

Two part long box,
6½"l x 2½"w x 2½"h.

Figure of cat lying down
covered with blanket, blue floral
decoration, blue bows.

$200.00 – 250.00.

Figural trinket box.

German, unmarked, c. 1910 – 1930s.

Two part box, 4¾"l x 1½"w x 4½"h.

Figure of girl, cat on lid.

$150.00 – 200.00.

Dresser box.

German, unknown mark,
c. 1930 – 1940s.

Two part box with
heart-shaped finial.

Portrait transfer of lady in
green gown, green heart decoration.

$75.00 – 100.00.

Figural box.

German, unmarked, c. 1890 – 1920s.

Two part black box, 4½"w x 4¼"h.

Adorable bisque kitten with blue bow perched on lid, another kitten's head protruding from bottom part of box.

$400.00 – 500.00.

Back view.

Open view.

Figural box.

German, unmarked, c. 1890 – 1920s.

Two part trinket box with figure of gray striped cat on lid, lily pads and frog on lid.

$150.00 – 200.00.

Open view.

Figural box.

German, unmarked, c. 1870 – 1890s.

Two part ribbed box.

Two reclining cats on lid.

$150.00 – 200.00.

Figural humidor box.

German, unmarked, c. 1900 – 1920s.

Figural box in shape of ball, 5½"w x 5"h.

Gray and white cat reclining under bottom of box.

$400.00 – 450.00.

Open view.

Figural box.

German, unmarked, c. 1890 – 1920s.

Two part bisque box, bottom in shape of shell, lid in form of white cat.

$150.00 – 200.00.

Back view.

Fairing.

German, c. 1890 – 1920.

Two part dresser box.

Figure of cat and mouse on lid.

$75.00 – 95.00.

Fairing.

German, unmarked, probably
Conta & Boehme,
c. 1890 – 1920.

Figure of cat, pink ribbon
around neck, two parts.

$200.00 – 250.00.

Side view.

Open position.

Figural box.

German, unmarked, c. 1920 – 1930s.

Bisque two part box.

Little girl's head, chicken in relief on lid.

$150.00 – 175.00.

Figural box.

German, unmarked.

Figure of black cat perched on orange
pumpkin, two parts.

$200.00 – 250.00.

European Boxes

Every country in Europe produced fine boxes. Some of the best are eighteenth century Royal Vienna and Capodimonte snuff boxes, but these are mainly in museums and private collections today. A number of nice quality boxes decorated in the Royal Vienna and Capodimonte styles are well suited to collections.

ROYAL VIENNA

The Vienna Porcelain Factory was founded by Claudius du Paquier in 1717. It was second to Meissen in producing hard paste porcelain. The company began producing cabinet ware derived from silver shapes decorated with Chinese motifs and exotic flowers.

Financial difficulties forced du Paquier to sell his factory to the state in 1744. At that time the Vienna mark, a shield incised or in underglaze blue was first introduced. It represented the banded shield from the center of the Austrian royal coat of arms (bindenschild). Viewed upside down it gave the impression of a beehive mark.

From 1747 to 1830 the decoration of Vienna snuff boxes was among the finest in Europe. Most had silver gilt mounts with chinoiserie, floral, and courting scene decoration. Toilet boxes were produced as well. In 1785 a Vienna traveling casket box was made with a variety of cosmetic boxes and bottles inside. They were decorated with floral cartouches and a dotted green ground.

In 1864 the Imperial factory closed because of industrialization and rapidly growing competition. Royal Vienna's stock was sold off to the factory's best painters and gilders who, finding themselves out of work, set up their own decorating studios and workshops.

Royal Vienna became a style in the late nineteenth century. Porcelain decorating studios in Europe copied the early Vienna style and produced some exceptional boxes. The better quality boxes had a center subject or portrait with ornate decoration on the bottom and sides. The most eagerly collected are those with portraits of beautiful ladies. Portraits of Marie Antoinette are the most popular. A number of doré bronze boxes were made with porcelain portrait plaques inset into the lids. These range in price from $300 to $600, depending on the size and quality of the painting. They were usually lined with velvet or satin.

CAPODIMONTE STYLE

Contrary to popular opinion, the Capodimonte style of classical figures and florals in high relief originated at the Doccia factory not Capodimonte. Carlo Ginori founded a porcelain factory in Doccia, Italy, in 1737. Some

Marie Antoinette. Postcard, Stengel & Co., Dresden #29204.

magnificent snuff boxes were produced at Doccia in the eighteenth century, including a box with cameo reliefs of classical emperors.

In the latter part of the nineteenth century, Ginori in Italy, Ernst Bohne in Rudolstadt, Germany, and Samson and Bloch in France created a variety of boxes in the Capodimonte style. The trademark used was a blue or black underglaze crown over an N, the old Capodimonte mark. Boxes were hand painted with mythological figures, Cupids, family scenes with landscapes in relief, cavorting Cupids, or with armorial crests. Grounds are white or all gold with white cloud formations.

Boxes were made in all sizes and shapes. Most of them were hinged and ranged in size from 1½ inches to 12 inches wide. Just as a Capodimonte

123

style cup doesn't exactly match the saucer, the top of the box is often quite different from the sides and bottom. Popular shapes include oval, quatrefoil, cartouche-shaped, rectangular, round, triangular, and six to eight sided.

HEREND

Herend Porcelain was founded in 1826 by V. Stengl. Around 1839 Mór Fischer bought the company and led it to fame with his reproductions of Chinese porcelain. At the Great Exhibition in 1851 at the Crystal Palace in London, the beautiful porcelain dinnerware and decorative items exhibited by Fischer were admired by all and brought world-wide recognition to the Herend company. Examples of early boxes that might have been exhibited were a bonbonniere with a fish design and a smoking set with a cigarette box with a scenic decoration.

Two Herend reticulated boxes with flower finials, c. 1930 – 1980.

Herend made dresser, writing, and cigarette sets to match their popular tableware patterns. Boxes can be found in the Chinese bouquet, Queen Victoria, and Rothschild Bird patterns. Many boxes are reticulated and have figural finials on the lids. These include flowers, strawberries, birds, rabbits, and other animals.

One reason collectors appreciate Herend porcelain is the amount of handwork that goes into each piece of dinnerware. Painters earn the right to sign their names on the base of each piece they decorate alongside the Herend logo. For collectors, such pieces are among Herend's most sought after items.

ROYAL COPENHAGEN

The Royal Copenhagen Porcelain Manufactory was established in Copenhagen in 1779. Financially supported by the royal family, Queen

Juliane Marie took special interest in its production. It was her idea to have three blue wavy lines, symbolizing the three Danish waterways, as the company's trademark. In 1868 Royal Copenhagen ceased being state-owned, and in 1884 the factory was moved from the city of Copenhagen to the rural suburb of Frederiksberg.

Royal Copenhagen produced a variety of boxes to match their famous dinnerware patterns. Its most well known pattern, Blue Fluted, is of Chinese origin and was created in 1780. It has three edge forms: smooth edge, closed lace edge, and perforated lace edge. It is still very popular today and is called the national tableware of Denmark. Another famous pattern, Blue Flower, was first designed in 1775. The blue bouquets are still painted by hand and include roses, tulips, poppies, and carnations. Each piece carries the signature of the painter. There are three different versions of Blue Flower: angular, curved, and braided.

In 1790 the company produced one of their most prestigious and oldest dinner services in production today, Flora Danica. It is still being made today. Flora Danica takes considerable artistic skill to paint the flora and takes more than 10,000 individual brush strokes to complete one box. Prices are high for Flora Danica boxes, from $700 to $900.

RUSSIA

Some of the rarest snuff boxes were made in St. Petersburg, Russia, in the eighteenth century. Today over 2,000 jewel encrusted snuff boxes are on display at the State Hermitage Museum in the heart of St. Petersburg. Many of the boxes belonged to Catherine the Great as she had a large collection of snuff boxes. The Imperial Factory came into its own during her reign, 1762 – 1792. She had a passion for buildings and for filling what she built with beautiful objects.

The M. Kutznetsov Company is a huge family porcelain business that had its beginning in 1842. In the early twentieth century, it eliminated so many competitors that it was responsible for about two–thirds of the total quanity of pottery and porcelain through the Russian Empire. It is still in business today. At the end of the nineteenth century they became known for their figural boxes. A two part fruit box in the form of an apple with pale pink enameled "skin" mounted on a leaf with a gilt handle ranges in price from $600 to $700.

SPAIN

A faience factory was established in Alcora, Spain, by Count Arendas in 1784. Two potters, Christobal Pastor and Vincento Alvara, were sent to study porcelain factories in Paris. They were especially interested in the French snuff boxes. The company achieved some important work and produced cream-colored boxes in the French and English styles.

Figural box.

Dwenger, C. L., Carlsbad, Austria, c. 1900 – 1917.

Two part box, 3¾" x 4¾"h.

Figure of an owl on lid perched on a branch, Imari colors.

$50.00 – 75.00.

Back view.

Dresser box.

Royal Dux, c. 1947 – 1970s.

Two part box.

Floral transfer, gilt decoration (see mark 83).

$75.00 – 100.00.

Trinket box.

Royal Vienna style mark, c. 1890s.

Hinged bronze box, original velvet lining, 2" x 1¾".

Oval porcelain plaque with portrait of lovely lady with long brown hair and a red cap after Asti.

$400.00 – 450.00.

Close-up.

Trinket box.

Royal Vienna style mark, c. 1890s.

Two part box, 3½"l x 1¾"h.

Hand-painted portrait of a lovely lady with a scarf, cobalt blue base with gilt.

$300.00 – 325.00.

Close-up.

Portrait box.

Royal Vienna style mark, c. 1890s.

Two part round box.

Hand-painted portrait Marie D'Anjou framed by gold beads, cobalt ground.

$200.00 – 250.00.

Portrait box.

Ernst Wahliss, Turn Teplitz, c. 1899 – 1918.

Two part box, 2½" x 1¾".

Cobalt blue with gilt decoration, beautiful hand-painted portrait of a lady with laurel leaves in her hair in the Art Nouveau style (see mark 107).

$225.00 – 250.00.

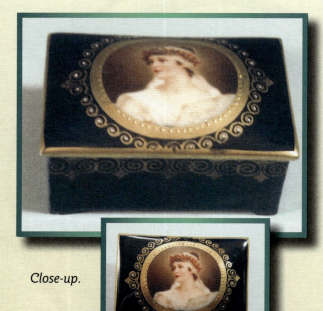

Close-up.

Portrait box.

Royal Vienna style mark, c. 1890s.

Oval hinged box.

Hand-painted portrait Marie Antoinette on lid, turquoise ground on bottom with gilt decoration (see mark 84).

$300.00 – 350.00.

Open view.

Another view.

Dresser set.

Union Porcelain Factories, Czechoslovakia, c. 1925 – 1939.

Set includes tray, three covered boxes, pair candleholders, ring holder.

Transfer decoration peacocks.

$200.00 – 250.00.

Trinket box.

Basco Company, Czechoslovakia, c. 1930s.

Hinged box.

Scene with carriage and horses (see mark 2).

$175.00 – 200.00.

Close-up of lid.

Snuff box.

Capodimonte style, c. 1870 – 1890s.

Hinged box, 2¼" x 1½" x 1¼".

Original brass frame, relief hand-painted cupids.

$200.00 – 250.00.

Close-up.

Snuff box.

Capodimonte style, c. 1870 – 1890s.

Oval, hinged box, 2¼" x 1¾" x 1".

Original brass frame relief hand-painted cupids.

$200.00 – 250.00.

Open view.

Trinket box.

Capodimonte style, c. 1890s.

Oval hinged box, 4⅛"w x 2⅛"h.

Head of woman in relief under clasp, figures of children, colorful (see mark 6).

$300.00 – 350.00.

Close-up.

Trinket box.

Capodimonte style, c. 1890s.

Hinged box.

Mythological figures in relief.

$250.00 – 300.00.

Trinket box.

Capodimonte style, c. 1890s.

Quatrefoil box.

Mythological figures in relief, gilt decoration.

$250.00 – 300.00.

Close-up.

Snuff box.

Capodimonte style, c. 1890.

Cartouche shaped hinged box,
2¼"w x 3½"h.

Raised figures in a forest setting
on top and side (see mark 7).

$400.00 – 500.00.

Open view.

Trinket box.

Capodimonte style, c. 1890.

Two part quatrefoil box, 4"w x 3 ¼"h.

Hand-painted relief figures of cupids
picking cherries and grapes.

$125.00 – 150.00.

Close-up of lid.

Casket box.

Capodimonte style, c. 1890.

Hinged box, 7½"l x 6½"w x 3½"h.

Hand-painted lady with four cupids in relief with golden cart on lid, colorful flowers and fleur-de-lis on sides and on border of lid.

$900.00 – 1,000.00.

Open view.

Close-up.

Casket box.

Capodimonte style, c. 1890.

Hinged box,
5½"l x 3¼"w x 2¼"h.

Relief cupids busy at different tasks, gold vase on lid.

$400.00 – 450.00.

Close-up.

Trinket box.

Capodimonte style, c. 1900.

Oval hinged box,
2⅞"l x 2⅛"w x 1¾"h.

Four relief cupids playing with a goat on lid surrounded by flowers, cupids and dolphins on sides.

$150.00 – 175.00.

Open view.

Trinket box.

Capodimonte style, c. 1890.

Round hinged box, 3¾" x 2½"h.

Relief painting of a maiden and Cupid on lid, colorful leafy design on bottom, two lush roses on inside.

$200.00 – 350.00.

Side view.

Trinket box.

Capodimonte style, c. 1890.

Triangular hinged box, 4"l x 2"h.

Cupid in relief picking grapes,
hand-painted rose inside box.

$300.00 – 350.00.

Another view.

Trinket box.

Capodimonte style, c. 1900 – 1910.

Six-sided two part box.

Mythological figures in relief.

$125.00 – 150.00.

Trinket box.

Ginori, c. 1920 – 1930s.

Two part cylindrical box, 2½"w x 3½"h.

Applied rose on lid, over-painted transfer of
courting scene (see mark 29).

$115.00 – 125.00.

Back view.

Dresser box.

Herend, c. 1930s.

Two part box.

Hand-painted flowers, applied peach rose finial on lid (see mark 32).

$125.00 – 150.00.

Trinket box.

Herend, c. 1980s.

Two part box, 2"d x 2½"h.

Reticulated chintz flower design, hand painted, white rose finial (see mark 33).

$150.00 – 175.00.

Trinket box.

Herend, c. 1980s.

Two part box, 2¾"w x 3 ¼"h.

Reticulated chintz flower design, hand-painted, applied strawberry finial.

$150.00 – 175.00.

Trinket box.

Herend, c. 1970 – 1980s.

Octagonal box, 2" x 2"h.

Applied rabbit finial, hand-painted blue flowers.

$125.00 – 150.00.

Trinket box or pot d'crème.

Royal Copenhagen, Flora Danica, c. 1969 – 1974.

Triangular two part box, 2¾" x 3".

Sawtooth edge lid with an applied branch and flowers.

Hand-painted pink flowers, on bottom (see mark 81).

$700.00 – 800.00.

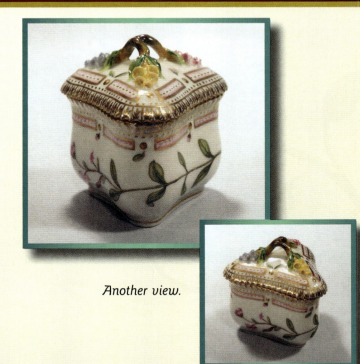

Another view.

Close-up of lid.

Open view.

Figural box.

Kuznetzov, Russia, c. 1890s.

Two part box in form of apple, 7" x 4"h.

Apple shape with pale pink enameled "skin," mounted on a leaf with a gilt handle (see mark 37).

$600.00 – 700.00.

Another view.

Figural box.

Unsigned, Russian, c. 1890s.

Two part box in form of pear, 5½" x 4"h.

Orange and yellow with an applied leaf as a handle.

$300.00 – 350.00.

Open view.

Trinket box.

Alcora, Spain, c. 1780s.

Faience hinged box, 4¼" x 3" x 2".

Scene of Joan of Arc in Orleans in under-glaze cobalt blue, rare (see mark 1).

$500.00 – 550.00.

Close-up.

Trinket box.

Spain, unidentified company, c. 1910 – 1920s.
Made special for Birks of Canada.

Cartouche shaped and hinged, 2¼" x 1⅔" x 1".

Cobalt blue with gilt roses, hand-painted
flowers on lid, flower finial and roses inside.

$125.00 – 150.00.

Close-up.

English Boxes

Although England is best known for their wonderful enameled boxes, some important pottery and porcelain boxes, were made as well. Collectors look for Staffordshire hen boxes, majolica sardine boxes, and early porcelain snuff, toilet, sweetmeat, and trinket boxes. A variety of lovely bone china boxes were made in the nineteenth and twentieth centuries by all the English manufacturers.

STAFFORDSHIRE HEN BOXES

During the late nineteenth century Staffordshire hen on nest boxes were very popular in Victorian households. They were used to hold hard boiled eggs and were often made in bright colors to decorate a table. The bottom part of the box was often done in a basketweave mold. Sometimes eggs could be seen under the hen. The boxes range in price from $200 to $600, depending on the decoration and color. They were made by a number of manufacturers in the Staffordshire area of England, and many are unmarked.

Staffordshire hen on nest box, c. 1850 – 1890s.

MAJOLICA

Majolica dates from Medieval Italy when it was an everyday pottery glazed with an opaque tin enamel in purples and coppery greens. It was in nineteenth century England that majolica appeared again. Herbert Minton started the craze, calling his brightly colored pottery with heavy relief nature themes "majolica." Then makers from all over England, Europe, and American started to turn out similar whimsical wares.

One of the most interesting boxes made of majolica is a sardine box. Sardines were a delicacy in England, but once opened the tin was greasy. The Victorian ladies wanted a beautiful vessel to serve them. A majolica sardine box with applied fish made by George Jones was valued at $3,300 – 4,125 at a 2007 Sotheby's New York auction. Other figurals made of majolica were tobacco boxes, match boxes with strikers on the bottom, and biscuit boxes. A rare majolica soap box has been found.

PARIAN WARE

Parian, a white porcelain made to imitate Italian marble, was made in the last half of the nineteenth century in England. Many small boxes were made in an endless variety of shapes and motifs. Some examples are birds in nests, lions, lambs, dogs, and sleeping babies. A few companies making parian were Copeland, Minton, and Mayer & Meigh. A tinted parian trinket box and cover with a sleeping child on the lid would be a rare treasure for a box collector.

POT LIDS

Pot lids are the covers of small pottery containers used to hold a variety of manufactured products primarily from 1840 to 1920. They were frequently decorated by transfer printing to describe the contents. They held hair dressing, potted meats, cold cream, tooth paste, anchovy paste, caviar, and bear's grease.

Many pot lids were produced simply to attract buyers for their products. Firms commissioned Staffordshire pottery companies, such as F & R Pratt of Fenton, Meyer & Co., Burslem, and Cauldran Pottery Co. of Shelton to produce the lid and container to advertise their wares. Lids are unhinged and loose fitting. They are mainly circular in shape, but some are rectangular. To most collectors, just having the lid is important and it can be framed and displayed nicely on a dining room wall. Most of the pots and lids are slightly damaged because many were thrown away in the trash when the contents were used up. Many were retrieved later in dumps.

Pot lids range in price from $100 to $200 and could go as high as thousands today. Those with strong colors and unusual subjects are the most valuable.

English Pratt ware pot lid box, "The Village Wedding," c. 1857.

MAKERS

COALPORT

"Perhaps the most remarkable thing about the boxes produced by Coalport was the number of different shapes used and the purposes for which they were designed." (Coalport by Michael Messenger, Woodbridge, Antique Collectors' Club Ltd., c. 1995)

Coalport's history goes back to 1750 when Squire Brown of Caughley Hill in Shropshire began producing pottery using clay and coal from his estate. When he died, his nephew took the business over. He was joined in 1772 by Thomas Turner. The firm was sold in 1799 to John Rose who had founded a manufactory at Coalport village. In 1926 Coalport moved from Shropshire to Stoke-on-Trent. In 1967 it became a member of the Wedgwood Group.

Coalport produced a variety of different types of boxes. Trinket boxes and casket boxes were common. Casket boxes were made in at least two different sizes. One was about six inches long, and the larger size was eight and one-fourth inches long. Coalport made dresser boxes, match boxes, and writing boxes. They were made in many different shapes and colors. They made square, circular, rectangular, oval, hexagonal, kidney, heart, shield, egg, shell, bellow, and bell shaped. Some boxes had gold feet.

Coalport star-shaped box, hand-painted scene, c. 1891 – 1920.

During the nineteenth century popular ground colors were celadon, pink, pale yellow, ivory, turquoise, and cobalt blue. Turquoise was used with a number of patterns based upon Far Eastern designs. The turquoise was sometimes overlaid with gold decoration. Cobalt blue was often used because of the great richness and depth of color that it suggested.

Some of the most desirable Coalport cabinet boxes feature gold and enamel jewels on gold ground. These jewels or enamel droplets were applied by hand. In addition to the fine jeweled decoration, some of the rarest of these cabinet pieces also have hand-painted cartouches with landscapes, birds, or flowers. Those that are artist signed bring the highest prices.

ROYAL CROWN DERBY

William Duesbury opened the Derby Works in Derby, England, in 1755. Perhaps more than any other English company, Royal Crown Derby was inspired by the Far East for their designs; it developed a great number of Imari and Persian style patterns. The company used rich, jewel-colored grounds of mazarine, cobalt blue, coral, and jade green ornamented with heavily raised chased gold. The designs were inspired by the birds, flowers, insects, and traditional motifs seen on priceless carpets and embroideries.

Royal Crown Derby made a variety of boxes in the Imari patterns, including cigarette, trinket, and pill boxes. In the late nineteenth century it produced bone china repoussé wares which were molded to give the impression of metal repoussé work. A heart-shaped box dating 1888 had this rare design. Royal Crown Derby made a series of miniature items in the early twentieth century including boxes. These are very popular with collectors.

CROWN STAFFORDSHIRE

Crown Staffordshire was established in 1833 by Thomas Green and remained in the Green family until 1964. In 1973 the company became part of the Wedgwood group. At the turn of the twentieth century the company was producing a wide range of bone china products including boxes. Many of the patterns had Oriental motifs with hand enameling. Most boxes were in two parts, but a hinged trinket box was made in 1914 with a hand-enameled bird in a flowering tree branch. It is valued at $150 – 175.

IRISH BELLEEK

David McBirney and Robert Armstrong founded the Belleek Pottery Company in County Fermanagh, Ireland, in 1857. Using local clay deposits, Belleek parian china was soon produced, which was extremely thin and light with a creamy ivory surface and pearl-like luster. Early Irish Belleek boxes are rare and desirable to collectors. A forget-me-not trinket box that is difficult to find in undamaged condition, a popular cherub box, and a rare clam shell box with a coral finial were produced. Trinket and cigarette boxes in their popular dinnerware patterns, such as Shamrock and Tridacna, were also made.

WEDGWOOD

The Wedgwood pottery was established in 1759 by Josiah Wedgwood in Stoke-on-Trent. He was born into a family with a long tradition as potters. Wedgwood produced a highly durable cream-colored earthenware that so pleased Queen Charlotte that she appointed him royal supplier of dinnerware in 1762. Wedgwood also developed revolutionary ceramic materials, such as basalt and jasperware. Josiah Wedgwood is credited with being "The Father of English Potters."

Boxes were produced by Wedgwood from the 1760s up to the present day, and early examples are quite rare. It produced patch boxes, etuis, snuff boxes, pin boxes, and sweetmeat boxes.

When Wedgwood began his experiments with jasperware, he could only fire small items at first. He created cameo plaques that were then inlaid in boxes of different materials. A rare Wedgwood sewing box was made 1785 – 1800. It was rosewood inlaid with dark blue and white jasperware cameos. The box measured 13¾"l x 10¼" x 3⅞". In 1780 – 1800 Wedgwood produced lovely patch boxes in ivory with tri-color Jasper dip cameos.

Go to Bed match boxes were popular in England in the mid to late 1800s. Most had a rough surface on which a match could be struck. They were made of metal, wood, ivory, pottery, and porcelain. They all featured a small hole or two in the lid into which a lighted match could be placed. A Wedgwood Go to Bed blue and white jasperware box is valued at $350 – 400.

Wedgwood "Go to Bed" match box, c. 1855.

Wedgwood also made boxes from Queensware, Terra Cotta, and Basalt. A very rare box would be a Dragon Luster which would sell around $800 – 900.

ROYAL WORCESTER

The Worcester pottery was established in 1751 in Worcester, England. It went through many changes in ownership during the next 100 years. William Kerr and R. W. Binns bought the firm in 1852, and the company experienced an artistic recovery. When Kerr left in 1862, the Worcester Royal Porcelain Company, Ltd., was formed. The restyled company made some of the finest porcelain of the Victorian era.

Royal Worcester made a variety of boxes, including a figural dresser box with a putto on the lid, c. 1920 – 1930s, figural match boxes, casket boxes, and many dresser boxes. In the late nineteenth century Royal Worcester produced blush items with lovely peach to pale yellow to cream grounds. Items had a velvety texture and were usually hand painted with flowers. Powder and rouge boxes were made in this style. Artist signed boxes are quite rare, and the fruit pieces are particularly desirable today.

The most valuable of all Royal Worcester boxes are the wonderful reticulated pieces produced by George Owen. One example is a silk box made in 1917 to contain sewing thread. Each hole was cut out independently by hand. A trinket box with a damaged finial made by Owen was valued at $6,000 – 8,000 at a recent English auction.

Trinket box.

Coalport, c. 1950s.

Egg shaped box, 1¼" x 1¾" x 1¼"h, two parts.

Ming Rose pattern (see mark 11).

$75.00 – 100.00.

Trinket box.

Coalport, c. 1891 – 1920.

Two part star-shaped box, 3¼".

Underglaze cobalt blue leaf decoration with gold band and rim, center star-shaped medallion of hand-painted lake and castle scene (see mark 10).

$400.00 – 450.00.

Another view.

Close-up.

Trinket box.

Coalport, c. 1891 – 1920.

Two part box, 5".

Rich cobalt blue ground with gilt scrolls and leaves, hand-painted landscape scene framed with etched gold.

$800.00 – 850.00.

Close-up.

Trinket box.

Crown Staffordshire, c. 1914, made for T. Goode & Co., London.

Hinged box, 4¼"w x 2"h.

Mottled cobalt blue ground, four petal cartouche with hand-enameled bird in a flowering tree branch (see mark 13).

$150.00 – 175.00.

Close-up.

Dresser box.

Crown Staffordshire, c. 1906 – 1929.

Two part box, 3"w x 1¼"h.

Roses and cobalt and gold
fish scale border (see mark 12).

$125.00 – 150.00.

Dresser box.

Crown Staffordshire, c. 1906 – 1920s.

Round box with two part slightly domed lid;
cream ground, lid with applied forget-me-nots.

$50.00 – 65.00.

Dresser box.

Grimwades (Royal Winton) Byzanta Ware, c. 1930s.

Two part box, 4⅓"w x 2"h.

Art Deco, dark blue luster ground, bottom decorated
with red and white flowers with lavish gilt,
lid has colorful red, green, white, and gold butterfly
(see mark 31).

$300.00 – 325.00.

Close-up.

Trinket box.

Parian, unmarked, c. 1890s.

Two part box, 4½" x 2⅔".

Molded grapes and leaves in relief on lid.

$75.00 – 95.00.

Pot lid box.

English Pratt ware, 1857.

Two part box, 4"d x 2"h.

Lid entitled The Village Wedding; what is unusual is the English Registry mark is printed on the jug in the foreground.

$125.00 – 150.00.

Open view.

Pot lid box.

Burgess's Genuine Anchovy Paste, c. 1890s.

Two part box, 3¼"w x 2"h.

$100.00 – 125.00.

Close-up.

144

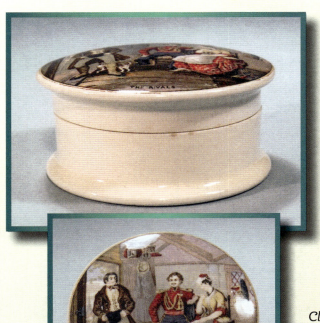

Pot lid box.

Pratt ware, 1890s.

Two part pot lid box, 4⅛"d x 2¼"h.

The Rivals.

$200.00 – 250.00.

Close-up.

Pill box.

Royal Crown Derby, c. 1902.

Two part round box, 1⅞" x 1"h.

Imari decoration (see mark 82).

$150.00 – 175.00.

Cheese box.

Shelley, c. 1940s.

Two part box.

Chelsea pattern (see mark 99).

$75.00 – 100.00.

Trinket box.

Spode, c. 1970s.

Heart-shaped box, two parts,
3⅛" x 3¼" x 1⅛".

Billingsley Rose Spray pattern.

$30.00 – 35.00.

Covered candy box.

Royal Winton, c. 1930 – 1950.

Footed two part chintz box.

Kew pattern.

$150.00 – 200.00.

Trinket box.

Tuscan China, England, c. 1932.

Commemorative box made for J. T. Allen, St. Martin's Lodge
#98, 2"d x 1¼"h.

Portrait of dog on green ground (see mark 102).

$100.00 – 125.00.

"Go to Bed" match box.

Wedgwood, c. 1850s.

Rare two part box, 3¾" x 1".

Blue Jasperware with white carving of goddess holding a dog on a leash, two holes in lid for stick matches, rim chips.

$350.00 – 400.00.

View of match-striking surface.

Close-up.

Pair dresser boxes.

Royal Worcester, c. 1898.

Round two part boxes, 3¼"w x 2¼".

Flower and leaf finials; velvety peach to pale yellow blush shading, hand-painted pink and yellow roses with forget-me-nots (see mark 85).

$150.00 – 175.00 each.

One of above.

Close-up of finial.

Trinket box.

Wedgwood, c. 1970s.

Square two part box.

Green Jasperware, mythological figures, floral border.

$50.00 – 75.00.

Dresser box.

Royal Worcester, c. 1914.

Two part round box, 2½"w x 1½"h.

Hand-painted robin in field setting (see mark 86).

$200.00 – 250.00.

Close-up.

Dresser box.

Royal Worcester, c. 1913, artist signed E. Phillips.

Two part round box, 3" x 2 ¼"h.

Hand-painted fruit and leaves, lush red apple and leaves in relief on lid.

$300.00 – 350.00.

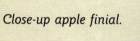

Close-up apple finial.

Dresser box.

Royal Worcester, c. 1901.

Round two part box, 2½".

Lovely blush ground with peach to yellow shading, hand-painted flowers with gilt (see mark 87).

$150.00 – 175.00.

Close-up.

Figural box.

English Staffordshire, unmarked, c. 1850 – 1890s.

Colorful hen on nest box, 5"w x 4½"h.

Green basketweave mold on bottom.

$400.00 – 500.00.

Open view.

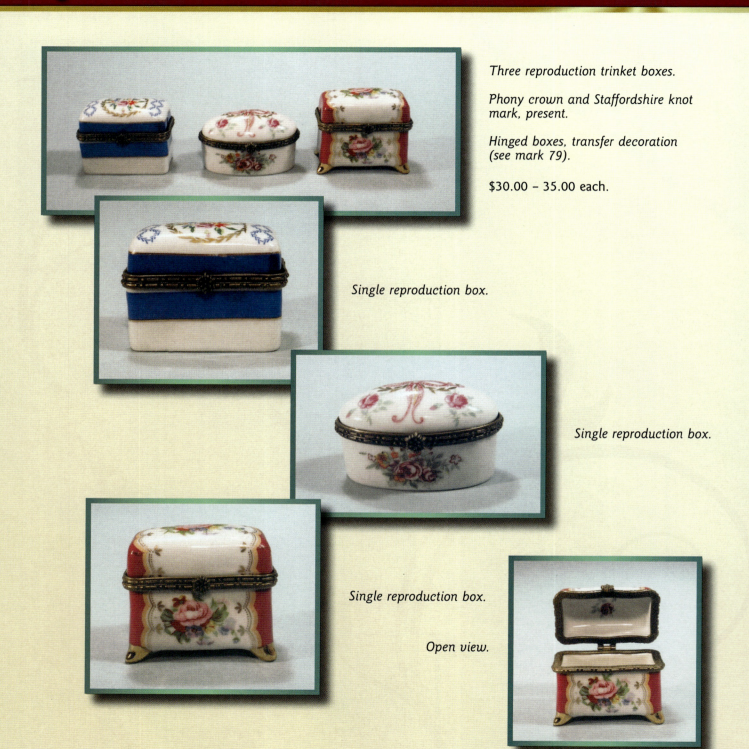

Three reproduction trinket boxes.

Phony crown and Staffordshire knot mark, present.

Hinged boxes, transfer decoration (see mark 79).

$30.00 – 35.00 each.

Single reproduction box.

Single reproduction box.

Single reproduction box.

Open view.

CHINA

EARLY DEVELOPMENT

The Chinese discovered how to make porcelain during the Tang Dynasty (618 – 907). They had a large supply of kaolin clay which was the major ingredient. The Chinese developed kiln techniques and the glazing processes and created the white translucent body known as hard paste porcelain.

During the Sung Dynasty (960 – 1278), porcelain production reached its highest point in terms of quality. The most important center of ceramic production was in the northern part of China, and white wares and celadons were the most famous. Celadon is a French term for the range of green colors, from deep olive green to a delicate sea green tint. Figural boxes have been found dating from this period, such as a lobed celadon box and cover modeled as a melon.

During the Yuan Dynasty (1279 – 1368) Jingdezhen became the center of porcelain production for the entire empire. Most of the porcelains had designs painted under the glaze in cobalt blue or copper red. The Imperial Porcelain Factory was established at Jingdezhen at the beginning of the Ming Dynasty (1368 – 1644).

By the end of the sixteenth century a variety of porcelain and pottery boxes were produced, including handkerchief, incense, sweetmeat, and game boxes to hold chess pieces. The early boxes came in a variety of shapes: round, square, and oblong with rounded ends. The boxes sometimes had interior compartments. Sixteenth century boxes were usually decorated with dragon designs in dark blue, often with touches of iron red. An example is a rectangular blue and white box with a domed cover having a pierced cartouche of Buddhist emblems and dragons.

During the Kangxi period (1661 – 1722) polychrome porcelains were produced as well as the important blue and white pieces. Boxes were made to hold brushes and paints. Perforated boxes were made to hold fragrant flowers.

CHINESE EXPORT

Chinese Export porcelain dates back to the late eighteenth century when it was introduced to the West by Portuguese traders from the East Indian Company. Porcelain manufacturing was still at the city of Jingdezhen. The population was more than one million, and 3,000 kilns were in operation. Much of the porcelain was sent to Canton (now named Guanzhou), where it was big business to decorate porcelain items for export to Europe and America.

The lovely Chinese porcelain was immediately successful. Especially sought after by collectors are items in the Famille Rose (pink palette) patterns. A few of the patterns include Rose Medallion, Rose Canton, Rose Mandarin, 100 Butterflies, and Tobacco Leaf.

Chinese pillow box, c. 1796 – 1820, blue and white flowers.

Chinese Export ware had three major designs in the eighteenth century: Oriental motifs, designs adapted from European prints, and armorials. Armorials were coats-of-arms of important European and American families.

Boxes in Chinese Export porcelain were predominately decorated in famille rose enamels, and subjects were emperors, scenes of tea ceremonies, figures, flowers, birds, and insects. Groups of stacking boxes, tea caddies, snuff, sweetmeat, and toilet boxes were made. Some were shaped like birds, shellfish, and flowers.

There were a number of boxes not made for export during the eighteenth century, including tea caddies, seal paste boxes, brush pot boxes, and pillow boxes. Pillow boxes are considered quite rare today. These boxes were used to store important family documents. Since most Chinese homes were not locked, the housewife would use the box as a pillow at night keeping it secure and protected. They were made of all materials, and wood was most common for the middle classes. The most beautiful and rare pillow boxes were used by wealthy merchants while traveling, and these were made of porcelain. A porcelain pillow box dating 1796 – 1820 with four different kinds of blue and white flowers representing the four seasons is valued at $3,000 – 3,500.

Chinese seal paste box, c. 1763 – 1795, cobalt blue scrolling lotus.

NINETEENTH CENTURY TO THE PRESENT

In the nineteenth century many boxes were still decorated in blue and white, but some had colorful overglaze decoration. Small boxes with landscapes had deep relief designs similar to red lacquer. The surface was usually covered with an opaque green or yellow enamel. Other popular motifs were street scenes, bamboo and chrysanthemum, scrolling lotus, insects, birds, children, and ceremonies. A hair glue box dating 1862 – 1874 had a pierced lid in the form of coins, hand-painted lotus, peony and prunus, butterflies, and crickets. The bottom part showed the Lantern Festival which is the fifteenth day of the Chinese New Year. This small box is valued at $1,500 – 1,800.

Chinese hair glue box, c. 1862 – 1874, Lantern Festival.

There was no hair gel in China until the 1920s. Men and women dressed their hair with a special glue. This was made by dipping thin slices of a special kind of wood into water that was placed inside a hair glue box. After an hour or so of immersion, the water becomes gluey and can then be applied over the hair, giving a shiny appearance.

A large variety of nineteenth century Chinese boxes can be found in the marketplace today, including pill, sugar, cigarette, hair glue, hors d'oevres boxes with compartments, and seal paste boxes. The use of seals originated in China 500 years BC. There were two categories of seals, official and personal. Official seals were issued by the Imperial Court for government use. These seals were symbols of power and nobility. All other seals were called personal seals. They were used for sealing up documents and were used on paintings and calligraphy works. The seals were protected in seal boxes. A variety of materials was used for making a seal box. Porcelain was considered the best material. An interesting seal paste box dating c. 1867 – 1874 has a hand-painted scene of five sons, showing a young rider achieving both civil and military honors. This round box is valued at $1,000 – 1,200.

JAPAN

EARLY DEVELOPMENT

The art of porcelain making was brought to Japan from China by Shonsui in the first half of the sixteenth century. The first kilns were established in the early decades of the seventeenth century at Arita. The first wares were produced in underglaze blue. Soon large quantities were shipped to Holland.

Ceramic techniques continued to develop during the next three centuries in Japan. Entire families worked in the pottery centers, passing their skills down to their children.

Following the reopening of trade with Japan by Commodore Perry of the United States in 1853, Japanese pottery and porcelain became extremely popular, attracting the attention of collectors. During the last quarter of the nineteenth century, Japanese influence played an important part in the Art Nouveau movement.

BANKO WARE

This interesting pottery originated in the late eighteenth century. It is characterized by thin, natural unglazed clay, hand modeling, and brightly colored enamels. Various marbleized or tapestry techniques were often used. Many Banko boxes are decorated with scenes from nature, such as cherry blossoms, bamboo, peonies, peacocks, and cranes. There were a number of interesting figural boxes with animals, birds, and various gods of good luck.

IMARI

Imari is the most famous name in Japanese porcelain. It was first produced in the seventeenth century in the secluded mountain villages in the Arita district of the southern Japanese island of Kyushu and was

Chinese seal paste box, c. 1867 – 1874.

guarded by samurai warriors to protect the secret ingredients. The earliest Imari was the blue and white ware called Arita. The clay had a high iron content making it good for firing at a high temperature. The finished products from the Arita district were often shipped through the port of Imari, from where they took the name.

At the end of the seventeenth century, overglaze red was introduced, and it rapidly grew in popularity. During the nineteenth century enamel decoration in multiple colors was popular among the wealthy Japanese who were the main buyers of expensive porcelain. Five colors, cobalt blue, pale blue, iron red, green, and gold, dominated. The complexity of design increased during the nineteenth century, and the ware became known as nishiki Imari or "brocade." Floral decorations dominate the center decorations, and the border patterns are derived from textiles. A variety of Imari boxes were made, including tea caddies, incense boxes, brush holders, cigarette, and trinket boxes.

Some examples found in the marketplace today are as follows: A blue and white obi knot shaped box, dating c. 1920s and measuring 8" x 4" sells for around $350. An Imari dresser box with a foo dog dating c. 1910 is valued at $400 – 500. A rectangular Imari calligraphy or brush box measuring 7¼" long with an overglaze painting of two high court officials surrounded by peony flowers is valued at $800 – $900.

KUTANI

Kutani means nine valleys, and the wares were first produced in the middle of the seventeenth century in a remote village in the Kaga province called Kutani. Kutani is distinguished by the use of five bold colors, in particular red, deep blue, deep yellow, purple, and green. The entire surface of the item is covered with colorful decoration. Themes include birds and flowers, landscape motifs, and geometric patterns. There is rarely a seal on the base of Kutani wares; however, the characters for Kutani, as well as the name of the artist, often appear.

Figural containers are among the most interesting of Japanese boxes, and many were made of Kutani ware. A figural box in the form of Hotei (one of the seven gods of good luck) emerging from his large sack, the lid portraying his face peering out, sells for $500+. A charming koro box or incense burner has a boy on each side of the box. Another interesting Kutani censer box is shaped like a quail.

NIPPON

Nippon identifies wares made in Japan from 1891 to 1921, rather than a single maker. After 1921 the word Japan was used. Nippon porcelain is highly collectible today and can be found with many different

designs and methods of manufacture. Many pieces are hand painted, and it is hard to find two pieces exactly alike.

At least 300 kilns operated in Honshu, Kyushu, Skikoku, and other provinces in the nineteenth century in Japan. Whole villages made porcelain and decorated it. Children were often used to help decorate Nippon. A tremendous amount of Nippon was exported to the United States, and there is a significant difference in quality.

A variety of Nippon boxes are available, including stamp, cigarette, and a variety of dresser boxes. They are decorated with moriage, beading, gold decoration, and hand-painted pagoda scenes, windmills, and florals. A rare butterfly-shaped powder box would be quite a find for a box collector.

SATSUMA

Japan has produced some of the world's most beautiful ceramic art, and Satsuma is one of the most distinctive. Resembling aged ivory, Satsuma is a soft paste porcelain, characterized by a fine creamy crackle glaze. The finely detailed hand painting and gold enameling is what makes Satsuma so treasured and sought after by discriminating collectors throughout the world.

Satsuma was first made at the end of the sixteenth century when a group of 17 to 20 Korean potters were brought to Japan by Shimazu Yoshirhiro, a general in the army. Satsuma was made continuously during the next two centuries. By the nineteenth century, potteries were set up in five major locations: Kagoshima, Kyoto at Awata, the island of Awaji, Yokahama, and Tokyo.

At the London International Exhibition in 1862 Satsuma was displayed for the first time in a Western country. From its first appearance, it was well received and in demand. When Satsuma became a popular export, the styles changed to suit Western tastes. Pieces became larger, and more colors were added. To satisfy Victorian tastes, raised enameling was used frequently in the decoration.

Some of the most valuable Japanese boxes available today are Satsuma kogos which are small boxes made to hold incense. They are usually round, quatrefoil, octagonal, or rectangular in shape and measure from 2½" to 3¼" in diameter. A kogo from the Edo Period (1790 – 1810) having a motif of a sixteen – petal chrysanthemum enameled in pale blue or cobalt with an iron red ground is valued at $1,000 – 1,500.

Kogos dating c. 1895 – 1910 were often decorated with flowers, figures, village scenes, and samurai warriors. The inside of the box also had decoration. These kogos range in price from $500 to $1,200+ depending on the quality of the decoration and maker.

Pillow box.

Chinese, c. 1796 — 1820 (Qing Dynasty Jiaqing reign).

Rectangular box, 9"l x 7½"w x 6¼"h.

Four different kinds of blue and white flowers on four sides representing the four seasons, old coin decoration on two ends.

$3,000.00 – 3,500.00.

Trinket box.

Chinese, c. 1723 – 1735 (Qing-Yongzheng reign).

Four deck box.

Blue and white scenes children at play.

$1,600.00 – 1,800.00.

Open view.

Medicine or pill box.

Chinese, c. 1875 – 1908 (Qing-Guangxu reign).

Cylindrical box.

Cobalt blue landscape.

$1,000.00 – 1,300.00.

Open view.

Sugar box.

Chinese, c. 1875 – 1908
(Qing-Guangxu reign).

Two part box or bowl, 4¾" x 5"h.

Cobalt blue and white hand-painted
street scene around body and on lid.

$2,500.00 – 3,000.00.

Soap box.

Chinese, c. 1875 – 1908 (Qing-Guangxu reign).

Two part box with pierced lid, studs inside box to
leave soap above water; famille rose, hand-painted
prunus, orchids, and fungus.

$1,100.00 – 1,300.00.

Soap box.

Chinese, c. 1875 – 1908 (Qing-Guangxu reign).

Two part box, pierced lid with knob finial.

Coral red with gold scrolling lotus around body, medallions
with fowl in bamboo and chrysanthemum in background.

$1,200.00 – 1,500.00.

Open view.

Seal paste box.

Chinese, c. 1821 – 1850 (Qing-Daoguang reign).

Two part rectangular box.

Famille rose decoration.

$800.00 – 1,000.00.

Open view.

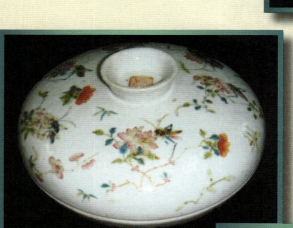

Hors d'oevres box or server.

Chinese, c. 1821 – 1850 (Qing-Daoguang reign).

Round two part box with knob, five compartments to serve appetizers or candy.

Hand-painted peony, prunus, and crickets.

$4,500.00 – 5,000.00.

Open view showing compartments.

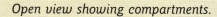

View showing mark.

Tea caddy.

Chinese, c. 1736 – 1795
(Qing-Qianlong reign).

Caddy, 3¼" x 4½"h.

Blue and white scrolling lotus design, red lid.

$2,000.00 – 2,500.00.

Cigarette box.

Chinese, c. 1875 – 1908 (Qing-Guangxu reign).

Cylindrical two-part box, 3½" x 5"h.

Gold fish in coral red.

$900.00 – 1,100.00.

Seal paste box.

Chinese, c. 1723 – 1735 (Qing-Yongzheng reign).

Square box featuring a cobalt blue cluster of flowers on top of cover surrounded by scrolling lotus and Buddhist ritual emblems on four sides to fit into container part of box below.

$2,300.00 – 2,500.00.

Open view. Note underside of cover has protruding edges on four sides to fit into container part of box below.

Seal paste box.

Chinese, c. 1763 – 1795 (Qing Dynasty).

Rectangular box with two sections to accommodate two pieces of seal paste.

Cobalt blue scrolling leaves and dragon head and butterfly design.

$1,200.00 – 1,500.00.

Open view.

Seal paste box.

Chinese, c. 1862 – 1874 (Qing-Tongzhi).

Round box.

Hand-painted scene of five sons, showing young rider achieving both civil and military honors.

$1,000.00 – 1,200.00.

Hair glue box.

Chinese, c. 1862 – 1874 (Qing-Tongzhi).

Rounded box with pierced lid.

Hand-painted scene of young man holding a petition board riding a fictitious animal called a kirin, led by his page and followed by a page carrying a parasol. (Only high ranking officers can have access to the Emperor to present petitions.)

$1,200.00 – 1,300.00.

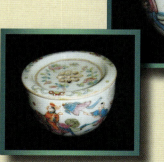

Another view showing pierced lid.

Hair glue box.

Chinese, c. 1862 – 1874 (Qing-Tongzhi).

Oval box, 2¾"l x 2"w x 4½"h.

Lid with two pierced openings in form of old coins.

Hand-painted lotus, peony and prunus, butterflies, and cricket; body showing Lantern Festival which is fifteenth day of Chinese New Year.

$1,500.00 – 1,800.00.

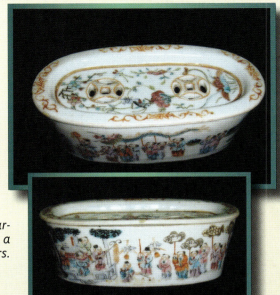

Another view showing children carrying lanterns and a child lighting a long string of firecrackers.

Another view showing a dragon dance with children playing musical instruments.

Seal paste box.

Chinese, c. 1920s (Hongxian reign).

Round box.

Hand-painted portrait legendary drunken poet Li Bai, terra cotta wine barrel on the floor.

$800.00 – 1,100.00.

Open view.

Rare four deck food serving box.

Chinese, c. 1862 – 1874 (Qing-Tongzhi).

Four decks, 6" x 7½"h.

Hand-painted flowers, fruit, bats, and birds; lid featuring peony and bird. (Four deck food boxes were to serve masters in chambers instead of formal dining rooms.)

$4,500.00 – 5,500.00.

Open view.

Another view.

View showing mark on bottom.

Seal paste box.

Chinese, c. 1763 – 1795 (Qianlong reign).

Round box.

Blue and white, scrolling lotus motif.

$5,000.00 – 5,500.00.

Open view.

Same seal paste box with desk size seal.

Covered ink box.

Chinese, c. 1890s.

Two part dagger shaped box, 5"l.

Blue and white design.

$800.00 – 1,000.00.

Trinket box.

Chinese, early nineteenth century.

Two part box, 2⅞" x 1"h.

Underglaze blue and white, hand-painted island and lake scene with two swimming ducks, tree in the foreground.

$150.00 – 200.00.

Seal ink box.

Chinese, 1862 – 1873.

Cube-shaped miniature box, 1⅛" square x 1" high.

Painted with Chinese figures.

$75.00 – 100.00.

Open view.

Seal ink box.

Chinese, 1862 – 1873.

Cube-shaped miniature box, 1¼" x 1" high.

Coral red ground with a painting of a bird and symbols in gold, paint flake.

$50.00 – 75.00.

Dresser box.

Chinese Rose Medallion, nineteenth century.

Two part box, 2¼" x 1½".

Decorated with three figures on lid, floral cartouches and figures on bottom, minor chips on rims.

$100.00 – 125.00.

Close-up.

Trinket box.

Chinese, Rose Medallion, c. 1890 – 1920.

Two part box; hand-painted figures and flowers.

$100.00 – 125.00.

Open view.

Trinket box.

Chinese, Rose Medallion, c. 1890 – 1920.

Two part barrel shaped box.

Hand-painted figures.

$125.00 – 150.00.

Back view.

Trinket box.

Chinese, Rose Medallion, c. 1890 – 1920.

Two part box.

Hand-painted figures and flowers.

$125.00 – 150.00.

Open view.

Trinket box.

Chinese, Rose Medallion, c. 1890 – 1920.

Two part box.

Hand-painted insects and flowers.

$100.00 – 125.00.

Trinket box.

Chinese, Rose Medallion, c. 1890 – 1920.

Two part box.

Hand-painted figures.

$125.00 – 150.00.

Back view.

Rouge box.

Ardalt, Japan, c. 1930s.

Round box, hinged, 1¾" x 1¼".

Original brass frame.

Decorated with a hand-painted bird and rose on lid.

$50.00 – 75.00.

Figural box.

Banko, Japan, c. 1900 – 1920s.

Two part round box, 2¾"w x 3½"h.

Cat in relief on lid, green on inside of box.

$200.00 – 250.00.

Open view.

Dresser box.

Imari, Japan, c. 1920 – 1930s.

Two part box.

Imari decoration.

$75.00 – 100.00.

Open view.

Incense box.

Kutani, Japan, c. 1900.

Six-sided two part box, 4½"w x 5½"h.

Figure of mother foo dog with her two babies on lid, Japanese figures in relief on side.

$250.00 – 300.00.

Open view.

Close-up of foo dog and babies.

Dresser box.

Japanese moriage attributed to Nippon, c. 1891 – 1921.

Scalloped two part box, 6"l x 3¾" x 2¾".

Allover colorful moriage with portrait of Duchesse du Monpensier on lid, floral car-touches on bottom, rare.

$200.00 – 250.00.

Close-up.

Dresser box.

Satsuma, Japan, c. 1920 – 1930s.

Two part box with three feet, 4¾"w x 2⅓"h.

Mille fleur design with a white chrysanthemum on the lid, lavish
gold decoration (see mark 88).

$125.00 – 150.00.

Card box.

Takahashi, Made in Japan, c. 1980s.

Two part box, slightly curved cover,
4¼" x 5½" x 2"h.

Phoenix Bird type pattern, three
hand-painted birds, vine work.

$35.00 – 40.00.

Small box.

Takahashi, Made in Japan, c. 1995.

Two part circular box, 2"d x 1¾".

Phoenix Bird type pattern.

$20.00 – 25.00.

Trinket box.

Japan, c. 1950 – 1970s.

Figural two part box, 8½"l x 6¼"w x 4¾"h.

Applied Cupid on lid,
flowers and moss (see mark 58).

$50.00 – 75.00.

Dresser box.

Japan, c. 1930s.

Fluted box with two part lid,
3¼"d x 2¼"h.

Hand-painted flowers, cobalt decoration on rim.

$30.00 – 45.00.

Contemporary Limoges Boxes

Contemporary Limoges boxes were first imported to the United States in the early 1960s. It was not until the 1980s that Limoges boxes were widely sought after by American collectors. Since that time the number and variety of boxes has increased dramatically. They can be found in upscale department stores, gift and jewelry stores, antique shows and shops, and they are sold on the internet.

Small hinged boxes are the most popular today. They range in size from one inch to three inches and come in many shapes. The boxes are usually hand painted with much use of gold. Prices range from $100 to $300 and more depending on the metal used for the frame and hinge and the quality of the painting.

The French phrase for hand painting is peint main. Contemporary Limoges boxes are painted by hand by an artist in Limoges, France. These artists are very skilled painters and spend at least five years as apprentices before becoming artists capable of painting Limoges porcelain. The artists use the same techniques that were used in the eighteenth and nineteenth centuries. Generally, boxes that are entirely hand painted are most desirable and sought after by collectors.

Today the technique of chromolithography or use of decals is also used. With this technique it is possible to reproduce up to 25 different colors on a special sheet, known as a design decal, which is manually laid down on the desired spot of decoration. Once this decal has been applied, it is then fired up to three separate times to ensure proper adherence of the design to the enamel.

Many contemporary boxes have the mixed decoration. The painting is added after the decal is applied to add emphasis to certain areas.

ARTORIA

Artoria is a family owned business located on the banks of the Vienne River in Limoges, France. It have been in existence for several generations. Artoria controls all phase of production. It produces its own porcelain and employs an extensive team of sculptors, artists, and designers. Artists at Artoria employ many of the same techniques that have been used by Limoges artisans for centuries to decorate porcelain boxes. It is the largest giftware manufacturer in Limoges and sell many of the box blanks to other studios in France as well as to companies all over the world.

Artoria has produced thousands of different Limoges boxes, and most of them are decorated by hand in its own factory. Each piece is richly detailed and signed and numbered by the artist. The boxes that are entirely hand painted only carry the mark Artoria and not the greenware mark. Artoria has a line of highly collectible boxes with Disney themes.

They are more expensive than other of the boxes because the company must pay royalties to Disney for the use of the name and characters. An example of a Disney figural box made by Artoria is a figure of Quasimodo holding a rod with a crown and wearing a royal robe from The Hunchback of Notre Dame. It is a Disney Limited Edition.

Limoges Artoria box of Quasimodo, from the Hunchback of Notre Dame © Disney, Ltd Ed.

Artoria made a variety of boxes including all kinds of animals, flowers, food items, and boxes representing the four seasons and the various holidays. They range in price from $100 to $300. Some examples include a gold muffin tin with six places for muffins and a knife clasp. It has a hand-painted cake server on the inside. Another interesting egg-shaped box has three monkeys sitting on top representing "speak no evil, hear no evil, and see no evil." It has a bunch of bananas on the inside and is valued at $150 – 200.

CHAMART

The company was founded by Charles Martine. The name is a contraction of Martine's given name and surname. Chamart was created in the early 1950s and was the first company to export Limoges boxes to the United States in the 1960s. It is still one of the major importers of quality boxes in the United States today.

Chamart boxes are completely hand painted. The blanks used by Chamart are made by other Limoges companies although many of the models are exclusive to Chamart. In 1965 Chamart introduced the Limoges box to the American market, designing a collection for

Tiffany & Company which was very popular. Good taste, quality, and the fact that each piece is hand painted is why Chamart is world famous.

Chamart boxes come in a wide variety of sizes and shapes and range in price from $100 to $300. The company is still in business today and is controlled by the founder's niece.

EXIMIOUS OF LONDON

While living in England in the 1980s, Josephine Louis discovered a charming and elegant shop called Eximious. The shop was famous for gifts and accessories, which inspired her to start a catalog and shop in the United States of the same name.

Louis and her staff have an extensive Limoges porcelain box collection which is the basis of her catalog and has come from artisans who produce unique and charming boxes throughout the world. Due to Louis and her staff's passion for discovering merchandise in the finest European tradition, her customers from around the world rely on Eximious to help celebrate any festive occasion with a wonderful choice of presents. Every item comes in an elegant box in her signature navy blue color and tied with a gold cord. Eximious of London is synonymous with good taste and elegance and has developed a clientele throughout the world.

Some examples of the boxes available signed Eximious are a hinged box with a hand-painted figure of a teddy bear sitting in a wagon with toys. It has a teddy bear for a clasp and is valued at $100 – 150. Another example is a hand painted figural egg with a flower shaped clasp. It is valued at $75 – 100.

ROCHARD

Rochard is one of the largest importers of Limoges boxes in the United States. It began operating in New York City in 1972 and is sold in upscale department stores and gift shops. Rochard worked with several small factories in France to create the twentieth century version of the Limoges porcelain box.

The Rochard Limoges box collection today has over 1,200 different styles including reproductions of the eighteenth century originals as well as contemporary designs. Representatives from Rochard return to Limoges, France, many times a year to develop new designs and patterns. Some examples are etuis, baskets of fruit, musical instruments, flowers, and egg-shaped boxes. They range in price from $100 to $300.

Limoges Rochard basket of fruit box.

LE TALLEC

Le Tallec is a decorating studio in Paris started in 1930 by the artist, Camille Le Tallec, who died in 1992. The company was subsequently purchased by Tiffany & Company in 1993. Using Limoges porcelain blanks, the company produced boxes, dinnerware, and decorative pieces. It owns 250 patterns, which are mostly interpretations of museum pieces from the eighteenth and nineteenth centuries. Tiffany & Co. owns some patterns that are made exclusively for it. Production dates, beginning with 1941, are marked on the bottom of each piece, so Le Tallec boxes can easily be dated.

Presently the Le Tallec studios managing director is Laureuse de la Grange. For the past 25 years she has strived to preserve the high quality and work and has helped with the creation of new patterns. Le Tallec is now owned by Tiffany & Company, although retaining its own identity. It continues to make boxes with the highest standard started by Camille Le Tallec in 1930.

It is easy to date a piece of Le Tallec. The pieces are marked with a L and T in script. The letters between the L and T indicated the year the piece was decorated. The letters under the L and T are the initials of the artist. When there are no letters to indicate the production date, the item was more than likely decorated during 1930 – 1940.

Prices for Le Tallec items are slightly higher than for other Limoges boxes as some are one of a kind and not available to the general public. Many patterns were made for a specific customer or company.

Contemporary Limoges Boxes

Prices range from $200 to $600, and some rare boxes are higher.

There are hundreds of patterns painted by Le Tallec, excluding the Tiffany & Co. Private Stock, of which some are exclusive to Tiffany & Co. Some of the Le Tallec original patterns were later modified and produced as commercial patterns. Several examples of Le Tallec patterns are described below.

Limoges Le Tallec egg-shaped box, Clairette pattern.

Limoges Le Tallec box, Cartes on Black pattern.

Clairette was created by Camille Le Tallec to celebrate the birth of his granddaughter Claire in 1982. The pattern is decorated in either pink or light blue with gold foliage. The Cartes on Black pattern has a painting of playing cards on a black ground. Oiseaux de Paradis depicts birds of paradise in various positions, such as flying, standing, and sitting.

The names of the most popular manufacturers of decorative boxes are well known, but there are other lesser known makers of Limoges boxes that made good quality boxes. A few of them are listed below:

Ancienne Manufacture Royal

Bernardaud Limoges — retails Limoges porcelain dinnerware and giftware

Carpenet — made dinnerware and gifts

Chanille — importer in the 1980s

Dubarry — located in the United Kingdom and produces Hand-painted and transfer boxes

Fontanille & Marraud — 1930s

La Glorietie — dinnerware

de la Reine — one of the oldest makers of boxes

Le Seynie — oldest box maker, taken over by La Reine

La Trefle — decorator studio

Parry Vieille — largest decorator

Figural box.

Limoges, Artoria, c. 1982 – present.

Hinged box, 3½"l x 1½"w x ¾"h.

All gold box in shape of muffin tin with six places for muffins, knife claps, hand-painted cake server on the inside (see mark 38).

$100.00 – 125.00.

Figural box.

Limoges, Artoria, c. 1982 – present.

Hinged box, 3½"l x 2¼"w x 3"h.

Hand-painted egg-shaped box with three monkeys sitting on top representing "Speak no evil, hear no evil, and see no evil," light green on outside, a bunch of bananas on inside.

$150.00 – 200.00.

Figural box.

Limoges, Artoria, c. 1982 – present.

Hinged box, 2½"l x 1¾"w x 2½".

Hand-painted dog and a ball on top of box, ball painted inside box (see mark 39).

$100.00 – 125.00.

Figural box.

Limoges, Artoria, c. 1982 – present.

Hinged box, 2½"l x 2"w x 3¼"h.

Figure of Quasimodo holding a rod with crown and royal robe, The Hunchback of Notre Dame © Disney, Limited Edition 473/1000; clasp shaped like a bell (see mark 40).

$200.00 – 300.00.

Figural box.

Limoges, Chamart, c. 1960 – present.

Hinged figural box, 1½"l x ¾"w x 1¾"h.

Pink teapot with yellow lid and blue finial
(see mark 41).

$150.00 – 175.00.

Figural box.

Limoges, Chamart, c. 1960 – present.

Hinged figural box, 2"l x 2"w x 4"h.

Figure of sitting rabbit with a rabbit clasp,
flower painted on inside (see mark 42).

$100.00 – 125.00.

Figural box.

Limoges, Chamart, c. 1960 – present.

Hinged figural box, 4"l x ¾"w x 1"h.

Figure of pea pod, intertwined heart clasp, pair
of red hearts on inside of box.

$100.00 – 125.00.

Open view.

Figural box.

Limoges, Chamart, current.

Hinged box, 2¼"l x 1"w x 2¾"h.

Hand-painted figure of woman golfer lining up her shot, golf ball claps, "Hole in one" on inside of box (see mark 43).

$100.00 – 125.00.

Figural box.

Limoges, Chamart, current.

Hinged box, 2"l x 2"w x 2½"h.

Hand-painted figure of Santa Claus in an airplane holding a Christmas tree and waving, Santa Claus face clasp, "Merry Christmas" inside box.

$200.00 – 250.00.

Open view.

Figural box.

Limoges, Chamart, late 1900s.

Hinged box, 2½"l x 2"w x 2½"h.

Hand-painted cat with a cup of milk, bow clasp.

$100.00 – 125.00.

Figural box.

Limoges, Chamart, current.

Hinged box, 1½"l x 1½"w x 3¾"h.

Hand-painted figure of a brown spotted seal balancing a green and white ball, fish clasp.

$150.00 – 175.00.

Close-up of fish clasp.

Egg-shaped box.

Limoges, Chamart, late 1900s.

Hinged box, 2¼"w x 3¼"h.

All gold with molded white/cobalt flowers.

$150.00 – 175.00.

Close-up.

Figural box.

Limoges, Eximious, c. 1982 – present.

Hinged box, 1½"l x 1¼"w x 2"h.

Hand-painted figure of a teddy bear sitting on top of a wagon with wheels and some toys, handle on box and teddy bear clasp (see mark 44).

$100.00 – 150.00.

Figural box.

Limoges, Eximious, c. 1982 – present.

Hinged box, 2 ½"l x 1¾"w x 1¼"h.

Hand-painted box in shape of an egg with attractive dark and light blue and green stripe, flower shaped clasp.

$75.00 – 100.00.

Figural box.

Limoges, Parry Vieille, current.

Hinged box, 2½"l x 1½"w x 3"h.

Hand-painted figure of a pelican in the process of eating a fish at the shoreline, painting of shoreline inside box, fish clasp.

$150.00 – 200.00.

Figural box.

Limoges, Rochard, c. 1972 – present.

Hinged figural box, 2¼"l x 1½"w 1½"h.

Hand-painted basket of strawberries with creamer and sugar bowl, spoon clasp, hand-painted strawberry inside.

$165.00 – 185.00.

Figural box.

Limoges, Rochard, current.

Box in the form of an etuis, flower clasp, 1½" x 2⅞".

Hand-painted stylized flowers with enameled vines and berries, bottom third all gold.

$200.00 – 250.00.

Open view.

Close-up.

Figural box.

Limoges, Rochard, current.

Hinged figural box, 2½"l x 2½"w x 2½"h.

Bowl of fruit in gold bowl, hanging cherries clasp (see mark 52).

$150.00 – 175.00.

Figural box.

Limoges, Rochard, current.

Hinged box, 1¾"l x 1¾"w x 3¾"h.

Figure of lighthouse, sailboat clasp, sea gulls on inside of box (see mark 53).

$100.00 – 125.00.

Figural box.

Limoges, Rochard, current.

Hinged box, 2½"l x 1¼"w x 1¾".

Figure of a violin and a sheet of music on top of box, music holder clasp.

$100.00 – 125.00.

Close-up.

Figural box.

Limoges, Rochard, current.

Two part box, 2½"l x 1½"w x 3"h.

Hand-painted box, replica of a Nantucket straw basket with an ivory plaque.

$125.00 – 150.00.

Figural box.

Limoges, Rochard, current.

Hinged box, 2"l x 2"w x 2"h.

Hand-painted figure of a cup and saucer with daisies on border, flower clasp, pink rose on inside of box.

$100.00 – 125.00.

Figural box.

Limoges, Rochard, 1972 – present.

Egg-shaped hinged box, 2¼"l x 2¼" x 3"h.

Hand-painted with cobblestone decoration with colorful dragonfly on leaf clasp, colorful figure of large frog inside box.

$100.00 – 125.00.

Open view.

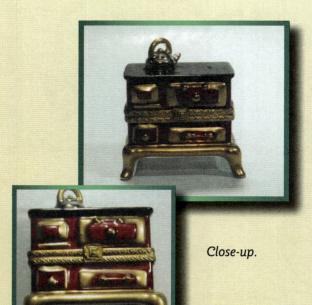

Figural box.

Limoges, Rochard, 1972 – present.

Hinged box, 2"l x 1¼"w x 2½"h.

Hand-painted box in shape of an old-fashioned red and black stove with a tea kettle on top, four legs.

$100.00 – 125.00.

Close-up.

Figural box.

Limoges, La Seynie, current, artist signed M. B.

Hinged figural box, 2¼"l x 1½"w x 2½"h.

Hand-painted figure of rabbit with polka dot egg, rabbit clasp, nest of eggs inside (see mark 46).

$100.00 – 125.00.

Open view.

Trinket box.

Limoges, Le Tallec, c. 1961.

Hinged box, 3½"w x 2½"h.

Insects pattern (see mark 50).

$350.00 – 400.00.

Open view.

Trinket box.

Limoges, Le Tallec, c. 1989, Tiffany Private Stock.

Heart-shaped box, 3⅓" x 1⅔".

Light magenta ground with hand-painted purple flowers and gold decoration.

$200.00 – 250.00.

Trinket box.

Limoges, Le Tallec, c. 1962.

Hinged heart-shaped box, 3½".

Corail Chinois pattern.

$500.00 – 600.00.

Close-up.

Trinket box.

Limoges, Le Tallec, c. 1962.

Hinged heart-shaped box, 2".

Cobalt blue with heart-shaped medallion with hand-painted flowers framed in gold (see mark 51).

$200.00 – 225.00

Close-up.

Trinket box.

Limoges, Le Tallec, c. 1945.

Hinged box, 4"l x 1½"w x 1".

Burnt orange with hand-painted leopard on lid.

$175.00 – 200.00.

Trinket box.

Limoges, Le Tallec, c. 1990s, Tiffany Private Stock.

Two part heart-shaped box, 2⅔" x 1¾".

"A Friend's Gift" on lid,
hand-painted red and blue flowers.

$150.00 – 175.00.

Cigar box.

Limoges, Le Tallec, c. 1966.

Hinged box, 3½"w x 5".

Garlands of hand-painted flowers tied together
with a bow, three gold medallions with hand-
painted roses (see mark 49).

$350.00 – 400.00.

Close-up.

Open view.

Trinket box.

Limoges, Le Tallec, c. 1968.

Heart-shaped hinged box, 2⅛"d x 2⅛"h.

Burgundy red ground with raised gold fleur-de-lis decoration.

$250.00 – 275.00.

Trinket box.

Limoges, Le Tallec, c. 1968.

Hexagonal hinged box, 2¾".

Grisgnan Vert pattern.

$300.00 – 350.00.

Close-up.

Coffret box.

Limoges, Le Tallec, c. 1982, made for Tiffany & Co., NY.

Egg-shaped hinged box, 4"l x 2½"w x 2¾", Clairette pattern.

$300.00 – 400.00.

Cigar box.

Limoges, Le Tallec, c. 1982, made Tiffany & Co., NY.

Hinged box, 3½"w x 4¾"h.

Deep royal blue borders on top and bottom with hand-painted pink flowers on front and white flowers on back, enhanced with raised gold leafy decoration, brass wreath clasp.

$350.00 – 400.00.

Back view.

Close-up of clasp.

Trinket box.

Limoges, Le Tallec, c. 1960.

Hinged box, 3½"w x 2½"h.

Hand-painted yellow flowers,
green and brown leaves on cream.

$175.00 – 200.00.

Trinket box.

Limoges, Le Tallec, c. 1990, artist signed J. P.

Round hinged box, 2" x 2½".

Cartes on Black pattern, red heart on inside of lid.

$150.00 – 200.00.

Trinket box.

Limoges, Le Tallec, c. 1968.

Heart-shaped hinged box, 2¼" x 1¼"h.

Oiseaux de Paradis pattern,
raised gold decoration on green.

$200.00 – 250.00.

Trinket box.

Limoges, Le Tallec, c. 1972.

Round box with domed lid, hinged, 2½" x 2¼"h.

Oiseaux de Paradis pattern.

$200.00 – 250.00.

Trinket box.

Limoges, Le Tallec, c. 1972.

Round box, hinged, 5¼" x 2½"h.

Oiseaux de Paradis pattern.

$300.00 – 350.00.

Trinket box.

Limoges, Le Tallec, c. 1970s.

Slightly fluted hinged box, 3"l x 2"w x 1¾"h.

Hand-painted butterfly and flowers, raised gold.

$150.00 – 200.00.

Trinket box.

Limoges, Le Tallec, c. 1960.

Heart-shaped hinged box, 2¾"w x 1¾"h.

Raised gold stylized flowers with cobblestone ground, all in gold and white.

$150.00 – 200.00.

Close-up.

Silent Butler box.

Limoges, Le Tallec, c. 1964.

Hinged box with a gold and white handle and leafy finial, 4¾" x 3¼" x 1½".

Beautifully decorated with raised gold paste stylized flowers on a rich cobalt blue ground.

$275.00 – 300.00.

Figural box.

Limoges, Vieille, Parry, current.

Hinged box, 2½"l x 1½"w x 2"h.

Nesting brown bird with long beak sitting on eggs, leaf clasp; flowers inside box (see mark 57).

$125.00 – 150.00.

Open view.

Trinket box.

Limoges, current.

Egg shape, 2½" x 1⅔" x 1½".

Hand-painted forget-me-nots and raised gold leaves.

$75.00 – 100.00.

Figural box.

Limoges, unknown decorator, artist signed Nogh.

Hinged box of lady's head, 2"l x 2"w x 3½"h.

Well defined face with grapes throughout hair, fleur-de-lis clasp.

$250.00 – 375.00.

Figural box.

Limoges, unknown decorator, artist signed M. C.

Hinged box, 1"d x 2¼"h.

Hand-painted beer stein, bow clasp, pump inside lid.

$75.00 – 100.00.

Trinket box.

Limoges, unknown decorator, current, artist signed P. V.

Hinged yellow rectangular box with pink roses on top, flower clasp.

$100.00 – 125.00.

Figural box.

Limoges, unknown decorator, current.

Egg-shaped hinged box, 1¾"d x 3½"h.

Figure of egg with hand-painted lattice work decorated with roses, crown on top of coat of arms clasp, inside complete tete-a-tete set, including teapot, creamer, sugar, and two cups and saucers, all decorated with pink roses.

$250.00 – 300.00.

Open view.

Figural box.

Limoges, unknown decorator, artist signed P. V.

Hinged box, 1¼"l x 1¼"w x 2½"h.

Hand-painted sitting elephant with trunk up, elephant clasp and a whip inside box.

$75.00 – 100.00.

Figural box.

Limoges, unknown decorator, limited edition.

Hinged box, 2½"l x 2½"w x 1¾"h.

Hand-painted cup and saucer in Sevres style, blue flower inside, flower hinge.

$75.00 – 100.00.

Figural box.

Russian, unmarked, current.

Two part bisque figural box, 2½"l x 2½"w x 3"h.

Light brown figure of spider across entire lid, green pock marked ground.

$50.00 – 75.00.

Close-up.

Open view.

Useful Information

There are many reasons why people start a box collection. Collectors old and new alike are buying boxes to decorate and beautify a home. A beautiful collection of antique boxes can help to brighten up a room. Some collectors consider antique boxes as an investment. Others buy to learn about antiques. Whatever the motivation for collecting boxes, it is fun and exciting.

GETTING STARTED

Everyone gets started collecting for various reasons, but you should make a plan before you start. There are some decisions to make before you start as to what direction you want to go with the collection. Boxes can be found in porcelain, bronze, silver, enamel, wood, or a combination of several of these. What material interests you? Do you just want hinged boxes? Do you have size limits? Is there a particular decoration you like, such as flowers or portraits. Do you want contemporary or only antique boxes?

A most valuable tool to start collecting is to buy a good marks book. This helps to date an item and gives you information about the maker. Talk to dealers at antique shows, especially a dealer that specializes in boxes. Visit a museum, and look at their collection of boxes. You may find them uninteresting, or you may be hooked. The marks on a porcelain box are extremely important to a collector. It will tell the company's name, and when and where it was made.

KNOWLEDGE

Knowledge is the key that opens the door for you. You should know how to determine the maker, and how old a piece is. Know the difference between the just average and the great, even those made by the same company. Know the difference between a decal and a hand-painted piece. The value of a hand-decorated piece is usually much more than a decal. It would be good to know the difference. It is a wise collector that can tell an authentic piece from a reproduction. It's helpful to know the age and rarity. Know how to examine a piece to determine its condition.

The knowledge you can gain from books on porcelain and porcelain manufacturers and antiques in general is unlimited. Each porcelain company has an interesting history of how it got started and the people responsible for it. This makes for some fascinating reading. You will be able to identify the different type of boxes and their shapes. You will know why one box costs so much more than another. With a good marks book you can tell when and where the piece was made.

AVAILABILITY

Porcelain boxes can be found in many places. Occasionally, a rare box can be found at a garage sale, flea market, swap meet, or house sale. You can add to your collection by buying at an antique show or shop. This is a way to talk to the dealer and ask questions about the items. It also gives you a chance to tell the dealer what you are looking for and how to get in touch with you if it is found.

Auctions are a source to add to your collection. You get to see and handle the box when you preview the auction items. It can help you determine the overall condition of the item. Remember it is the buyer's responsibility to check for the condition of a piece.

INTERNET BUYING

Everyone knows that internet buying has changed the antique business. For better or worse, it's here to stay. Buying and selling from the comfort of your own home with all your reference material and access to a world-wide market is a big advantage.

Internet buying also has a down side. The best way to buy anything, especially antiques, is to have a "hands on" inspection. Buying from a photograph and sometimes a bad picture at that, and a short description is a poor method at best, but it has significantly changed the way we buy and sell antiques.

Although it has been talked about many times in various mediums, we feel the need to repeat some of the hazards again, especially for new buyers and sellers.

One of the problems with buying on the internet is that some sellers don't have a good knowledge of what they are selling and also have a hard time describing an item. A buyer must sometimes read between the lines. Do not be afraid to ask the seller questions before you decide to make your purchase. It is sometimes too late after you receive the merchandise. A buyer should know the return policy of the seller. Certain conditions can be missed, such as if the item is sold "as is" and "cannot be returned" or "only if the item is not as described." If there is any doubt about an item, *don't buy it.*

When buying on the internet, consider the postage cost. The United States Postal Service is always increasing the rates. This has to be added to the buyer's winning bid price. Some sellers charge a handling fee to cover the cost of materials and their time. If the rate seems too high, you can challenge it.

PACKAGING

A tremendous problem that is often overlooked with internet buying and selling is the packaging and shipping of the item. Proper shipping is not just the responsibility of the seller. Buyers need to know how to pack as well. Occasionally a package may have to be returned to the seller for one reason or another, and it should be packed with care.

A shipper's first consideration is finding good sturdy boxes. It's okay to re-use a cardboard box if it's in good condition. All the old tape and tags should be removed. The box should be big enough to hold the item, and yet small enough so that it can be fitted into an outer box. Some boxes are fragile and should be double boxed. There should be space enough to encase the item completely in the box, top and bottom and on all sides. It makes little sense to put the item in a box and not cover the top and bottom, as these are the most vulnerable areas. A layer on top and bottom are just as important as the sides. Remember, the top and bottom have to be protected by more than a thin layer of cardboard.

Styrofoam peanuts are good to use as they offer a lot of protection and are light in weight. Paper offers good protection if enough is used, but it weighs much more than the peanuts. Shredded paper is fine as long as you don't have to be the one who opens the package, as it makes quite a mess. Boxes should be wrapped in bubble wrap, and enough should be used to protect the item.

Many shippers think that the more tape used to encase the item, the more the item is protected. This is not the case. A small piece of scotch or masking tape is enough to keep the bubble wrap in place on the item. Sometimes there is so much clear tape on the piece, it has to be cut off. This could cause some damage to the item itself.

Proper packing could eliminate a lot of unnecessary problems. Filing a damage claim is a hassle, and it takes a long time to receive the insurance money. The focus of the shipper is to have the package arrive to its destination safely. A lost antique is a loss to the world forever.

CONDITION

The condition of your box is of great importance. Listed below are some of the common things to keep in mind when you receive a box in the mail.

CHIPS

Porcelain is very vulnerable to chips. Run your finger around the item, especially the edges of the box and feel for any chips.

HAIRLINES

Hairlines are sometimes impossible to see. You can detect them with a jeweler's loupe.

WEAR

Gilt ware is very common on antique boxes, especially those made in the eighteenth century, and a small amount is acceptable to most buyers. Ground ware is more serious and very hard to repair as it's almost impossible to match the color. If the gilt or ground ware is excessive, it could take away from the appearance. It depends on the age and rarity of the piece.

HARDWARE

One of the unique features of boxes is the hardware which is the hinge, binding, and clasp. It has been a common practice for the porcelain box makers to have the metal work done by goldsmiths. The metal frame, hinge, and clasp on a box should be in good condition. Check to make sure the frame is completely attached to the box, that the clasp is intact, and that the box closes tightly and evenly.

RESTORATION

Just a few words on restoring a damaged antique. Unless you are very talented in this area, you shouldn't attempt it. Nothing looks worse than a badly glued piece or one that has been "touched up" with paint. A good restorer is hard to find and is expensive. If a seller tells you, "It's easy to fix," ask yourself, "If it's so easy to fix, why didn't he/she fix it?" A good policy is to not buy anything that is not in near perfect condition.

PROTECTION

As your collection gets larger and more valuable, you should think about getting some kind of insurance. It's an expense, but so would your loss be in a fire or if someone robbed you.

Look into the possibility of adding a Fine Arts rider to your homeowner's insurance policy. You many need an outside appraiser to determine the value of your antiques. If so, make sure you get the service of a qualified appraiser with recognized credentials. Any antique dealer may be able to recommend one, or you can find one in the telephone book in the yellow pages.

RECORD KEEPING

As your collection grows, it will be hard to remember what you paid for a given item and when you acquired it. If you have computer skills, you can list your entire inventory, and put it on a floppy disc for safekeeping.

If a computer is not your "cup of tea," another way to keep track of your collection is to photograph it. This could also be valuable for insurance purposes.

MARKS

1. Alcora, Spain, c. 1780s.

2. Basco Co., Czechoslovakia, c. 1930s.

3. Bavaria, unidentified mark.

4. Blois, Ulysse, c. 1932.

5. Borgfeldt & Sons Importer, Germany, c. 1920 – 1930s.

6. Capodimonte style, c. 1890s.

7. Capodimonte style, c. 1890s.

8. Chantilly, c. 1770 – 1790.

9.Chaufraisse, Marcel, c. 1930s.

10. Coalport, c. 1891 – 1920s.

11. Coalport, c. 1950s.

12. Crown Staffordshire, c. 1906 – 1929.

13. Crown Staffordshire, c. 1914,
made for T. Goode & Co., London.

14. Dresden, Donath & Co., c. 1890s.

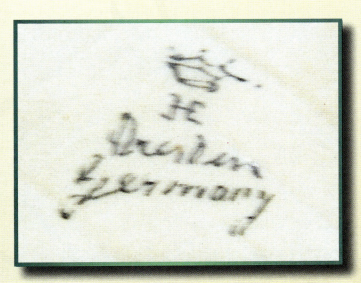

15. Dresden, Hirsch, Franziska, c. 1890s.

16. Dresden, Hirsch, Franziska, c. 1893 – 1920.

17. Dresden, Hutschenreuther, c. 1900 – 1920.

18. Dresden, Hutschenreuther, c. 1918 – 1945.

19. Dresden, Klemm, Richard, c. 1900 – 1920s.

20. Dresden, Koch, Wilhelm, c. 1928 – 1949

21. Dresden, Lamm, Ambrosius, c. 1885 – 1890s.

22. Dresden, Lamm, Ambrosius, c. 1890s.

23. Dresden, Thieme, Carl, c. 1920 – 1930s.

24. Dresden, Wehsner, Richard, c. 1890s.

25. Dresden, Wolfsohn, Helena, c. 1886 – 1891.

26. Dresden, Wolfsohn, Helena, c. 1890s.

27. Elfinware, Orben, Knabe & Co., c. 1910 – 1930s.

28. Februrier, Jacques Manufacturing, Lille, c. 1763.

29. Ginori, c. 1920 – 1930s.

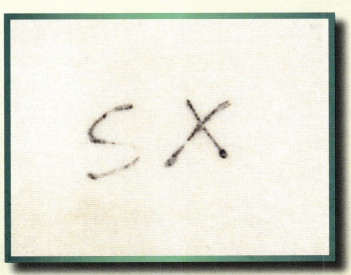

30. Glot, Richard, Seaux, c. 1770s.

31. Grimwades (Royal Winton), Byzanta Ware, c. 1930s.

32. Herend, c. 1930s.

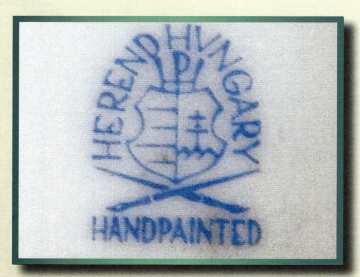

33. Herend, c. 1980s.

34. Heubach, c. 1890 – 1920s.

35. KPM Berlin, c. 1920s.

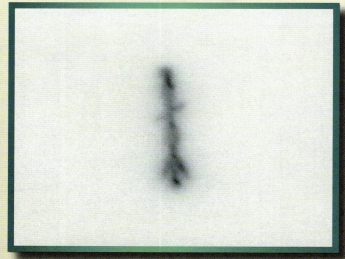

36. KPM, c. 1890s.

37. Kutznetsov, Russia, c. 1890s.

38. Limoges, Artoria, c. 1982 – present.

39. Limoges, Artoria, c. 1982 – present.

40. Limoges, Artoria, c. 1982 – present,
©Disney, Limited Edition.

41. Limoges, Chamart, c. 1960 – present.

42. Limoges, Chamart, c. 1960 – present.

43. Limoges, Chamart, current.

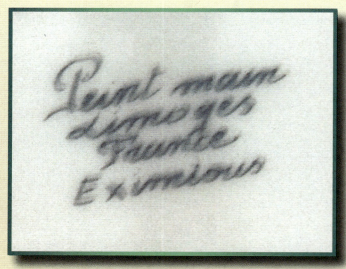

44. Limoges, Eximious, c. 1982 – present.

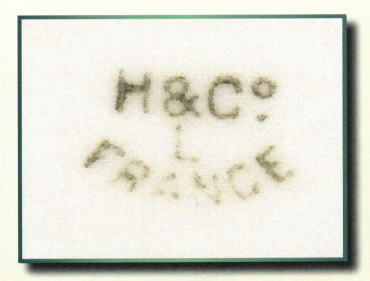

45. Limoges, Haviland, c. 1876 – 1930.

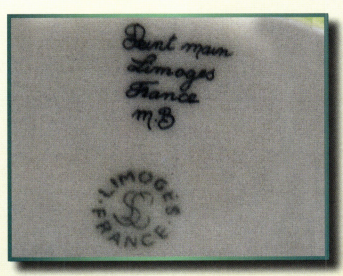

46. Limoges, La Seynie, current, artist signed M. B.

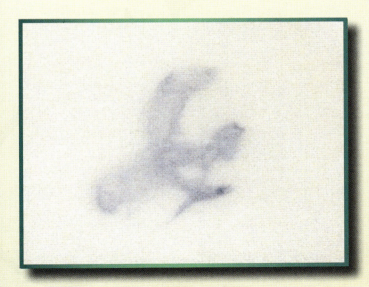

47. Limoges, Laporte, Raymond, c. 1860 – 1970s.

48. Limoges, Le Tallec, c. 1945.

49. Limoges, Le Tallec, c. 1966.

50. Limoges, Le Tallec, Tiffany Private Stock, c. 1961.

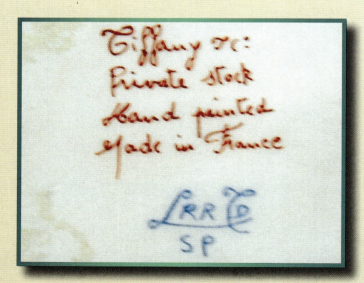

51. Limoges, Le Tallec, Tiffany Private Stock, c. 1962.

52. Limoges, Rochard, c. 1972 – present.

53. Limoges, Rochard, current.

54. Limoges, Tresseman & Voigt, c.
1892 – 1907, made for Burley & Co., Chicago.

55. Limoges, unidentified company, c. 1900 – 1930s.

56. Limoges, unidentified company, c. 1950s.

57. Limoges, Vieille, Parry, current.

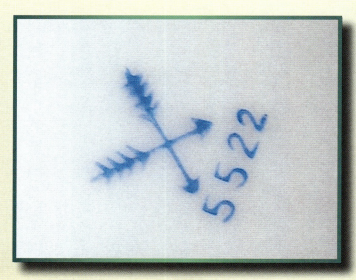

58. Made in Japan mark, c. 1950 – 1970s.

59. Meissen, c. 1850 – 1924.

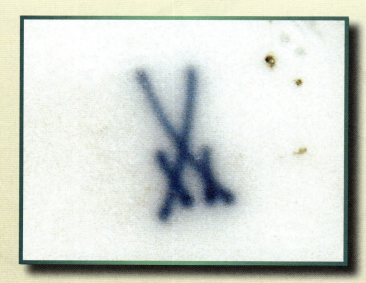

60. Meissen, c. 1953 – 1957.

61. *Nymphenburg, c. 1920 – 1930s.*

62. *Paris, Bloch & Cie, c. 1887 – 1900.*

63. *Paris, Bloch, Achille, c. 1920 – 1960.*

64. *Paris, Bourdois & Bloch, c. 1890 – 1900.*

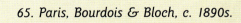
65. *Paris, Bourdois & Bloch, c. 1890s.*

66. Paris, Bourdois & Bloch, c. 1900 – 1920.

67. Paris, Bourdois & Bloch, c. 1920s.

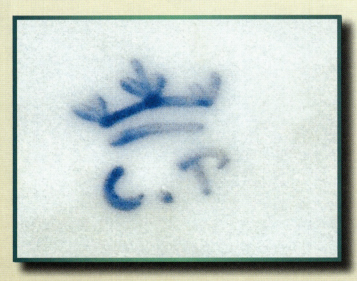

68. Paris, Fauberg St. Denis, c. 1830.

69. Paris, Milet, Paul & Fils, c. 1866 – 1941.

70. Paris, Pouyat & Russinger, c. 1808 – 1825.

71. Paris, Pouyat Bros., Rue Fontaine-ai-roi, c. 1808 – 1825.

72. Paris, Ruh-Leprince, Arnold, c. 1890s.

73. Paris, Samson, c. 1873 – 1876.

74. Paris, Samson, c. 1876 – 1884.

75. Paris, Samson, c. 1890 – 1910, fake Chantilly mark.

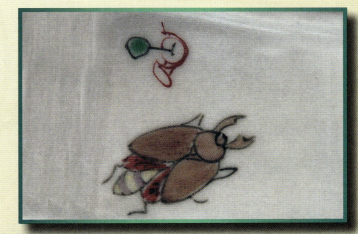

76. Paris, Samson, c. 1890s.

77. Paris, Samson, c. 1900, fake Chantilly mark.

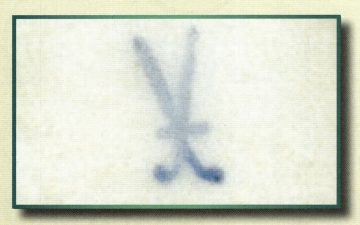

78. Paris, unidentified mark, c. 1890s.

79. Reproduction mark, phony
Crown & Staffordshire knot, present.

80. Royal Bayreuth, c. 1902 – 1920.

81. Royal Copenhagen, Flora Danica, c. 1969 – 1974.

82. Royal Crown Derby, c. 1902.

84. Royal Vienna style, c. 1890s.

83. Royal Dux, c. 1947 – 1970s.

85. Royal Worcester, c. 1898.

86. Royal Worcester, c. 1914.

87. Royal Worcester, c.1901.

88. Satsuma, Japan, c. 1920 – 1930s.

89. Sevres style, c. 1850 – 1860s.

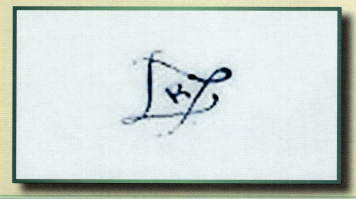

90. Sevres style, c. 1850s.

91. Sevres style, c. 1870 – 1890.

92. Sevres style, c. 1870 – 1890.

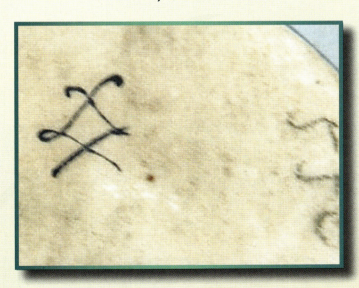

93. Sevres style, c. 1880 – 1890s.

94. Sevres style, c. 1890s.

95. Sevres style, c. 1890s.

96. Sevres, c. 1772.

97. Sevres, c. 1800 – 1810.

98. Sevres, c. 1804 – 1809.

99. Shelley, c. 1940s.

100. Sitzendorf, c. 1900 – 1910.

101. Teichert Co., Meissen, c. 1864 – 1900.

102. Tuscan China, c. 1932.

103. Veuve Perrin, Marseilles, c. 1760s.

104. Volkstedt, c. 1787 – 1800.

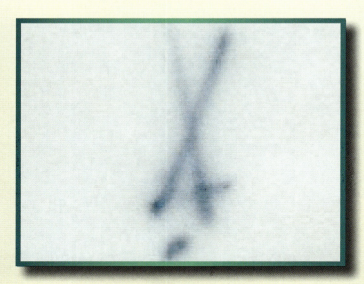

105. Volkstedt, c. 1870s.

106. Von Schierholz, c. 1907 – 1930s.

107. Wahliss, Ernst, c. 1899 – 1918.

Andacht, Sandra. *Treasury of Satsuma*. Des Moines, Iowa: Wallace & Homestead, 1981.

Ashford, Roger. "English Vesta Boxes." *The Antiques Journal*, September 1979.

Bagdade, Susan & Al. *Warman's English & Continental Pottery & Porcelain* Iola, WI: KP Books, 2004.

Baker, Myrtle, V. "Figural Powder Boxes," *The Antique Trader Annual of Articles Vol. X*, 1979.

Beaucamp-Markowsky, Barbara. *Collection of 18th C. Porcelain Boxes*. Amsterdam, The Netherlands: Rijksmuseum, c. 1988.

Berges, Ruth. *From Gold to Porcelain*. South Brunswick, NJ: Thomas Yoseloff, 1963.

Berkey, Richard L. "Hair Receivers for Treasures of the Heart," *Antique Trader*, 10/21/98

Bourne, Ursula. *Snuff*. England: Sire Publications, 1990.

Buten, David. *18th Century Wedgwood*. New York: A Main Street Press Book, 1980.

Cole, Brian. *Boxes*. Rador, PA: Chilton Book Company, 1976.

Danckert, Ludwig. *Directory of European Porcelain*. London: N.A.G. Press, Ltd., 1981.

du Tertre, Nancy. *The Art of the Limoges Box*. New York: Harry N. Abrams, Inc., 2003.

Furio, Joanne. *The Limoges Porcelain Box*. New York: Lake Warren Press, 1998.

Gaston, Mary Frank. *The Collector's Encyclopedia of Limoges Porcelain*, Vol. I and II. Paducah, KY: Collector Books, 1980 and 1992.

Godden, Geoffrey. *Encyclopedia of British Pottery and Porcelain Marks*. London, England: Barrie & Jenkins, 1986, 1991.

_____ *Godden's Guide to English Porcelain*. Radnor, PA: Wallace-Homestead, 1992.

_____ *Godden's Guide to European Porcelains*. New York: Cross River Press, 1993.

Harran, Jim and Susan. *Collectible Cups & Saucers Book I, II, III, IV*. Paducah, KY: Collector Books, 1998 – 2003.

_____ *Dresden Porcelain Studios*. Paducah, KY: Collector Books, 2002.

_____*Decorative Plates*. Paducah, KY: Collector Books, 2008.

_____ *Meissen Porcelain*. Paducah, KY: Collector Books, 2006.

Helliwell, Stephen. *Collecting Small Silverware*. Oxford, England: Phaidon-Christies Ltd., 1988.

"Hoe Snuff Boxes Sell for $18,415," *NY Times*, Feb. 26, 1911.

Huxford, Sharon and Bob. *Schroeder's Antiques Price Guide*. Paducah, KY: Collector Books, 2008.

Kamm, Dorothy. *American Painted Porcelain*. Norfolk, VA: Antique Trader Books, 1999.

Kaplan, Arthur Guy and Thompson, Rebecca P. "Chatelaines," *Spinning Wheels's Antiques for Women*. Hanover, PA: Everybody's Press, 1974.

Ketchum, William C. Jr. *Boxes*. Cooper-Hewett Museum, The Smithsonian Institution, 1982.

Klamkin, Marian. *The Collector's Book of Boxes*. New York: Dodd, Mead & Co., 1970.

Kovel, Ralph and Terry. *Kovels' Antiques & Collectibles Price List*. New York: Crown Publishers, 1992 Edition.

_____ *Kovels' New Dictionary of Marks*. New York, New York: Crown Publisher, Inc., 1986.

London, Rena. "Elfinware," *Antique Trader*, 6/4/80.

Mackay, James. *An Encyclopedia of Small Antiques*. New York: Harper & Row, 1975.

Marion, Frieda. "Figural Dresser Boxes," *The Antique Journal*, April 1978.

_____"Prima Donna Gathers Rare Snuff-Boxes," *Hobbies*, October 1937.

McClinton, Katharine Morrison. *A Handbook of Popular Antiques*. New York: Bonanza Books, 1966.

Bibliography

"Objets de Vertu," *Discovering Antiques*. New York: Greystone Press, 1973.

Poese, Bill. "Snuff and Snuffboxes." *The Antique Journal*, 4/71.

Rapaport, Ben, "The Four Hundred Year Transition: From Tobacco Box and Jar to a Pocket Roll Pouch," *The Antique Trader Annual of Articles Vol. VI*, 1976.

Ray, Marcia. *Collectible Ceramics*. New York: Crown Publishers, Inc., 1974.

Sandon, John. *Starting to Collect Antique Porcelain*. Woodbridge, England: Antique Collectors Club Ltd., 1997.

Savill, Rosalind. *The Wallace Collection Catalogue of Sevres Porcelain II*. London: The Turstees of the Wallace Collection, 1988.

Simpson, Richard. "Luxury Boxes for Vanity and Pleasure," *Antiques & Collecting*, February 2003.

Strumpf, Faye. *Limoges Boxes*. Iola, WI: Krause Publications, 2000.

Van Patten, Joan, *The Collector's Encyclopedia of Nippon Porcelain*, Vols. 2 & 3, Collector Books, 1982.

Vogel, Janice & Richard. *Victorian Trinket Boxes*. Ocala, FL: Pobneck Publishing Co., 1996.

Waterbrook-Clyde, Keith & Thomas. *The Decorative Art of Limoges Porcelain & Boxes*. Atglen, PA: Schiffer Publishing Ltd., 1999.

_____ "Limoges Porcelain," *Antique Trader*, Jan. 26, 2000.

"About Limoges Boxes." Limoges Outlet, www.limogesoutlet.com/

"Authentic Limoges Box Markings." French Porcelain Box Collection, France. www.limogesboutique.com/bear-figurines.html.

"Bonbonnieres," Antiques Digest-Lost Knowledge form the Past. Old and Sold Antique Auction & Marketplace. www.oldandsold.com/articles02/article1154.shtml.

"Casket," The Free Dictionary by Farlex. www.thefreedictionary.com/casket.html

"Chinese Document or "Pillow" boxes." Chinese Culture: Chinese Document Boxes. www.qi-journal.com/Culture.asp?-token.SearchID=Chinese%20Document%20Boxes

"Collecting British Polychrome Pot Lids, Jars & Wares. www.gostar.com/antiquing/potlids.htm

"Decorative Boxes," Wikipedia, the Free Encyclopedia. www.en.wikipedia.org/wiki/Decorative_boxes.html

"Great Books Online," Barleby.com. www.barleby.com/cgi-bin/texis/webinator/salesearch?filter=co/Quotations&Query=.html

"History of Limoges, France." Artoria-Limoges.com. www.artoria-Limoges.com/history1.html

"La Manufacutre de Sevres." Manufacture Nationale de Sevres. www.manufacturedesevres.culture.gouv.fr/site.php?type=P&id=56

"Limoges." About.com: Collectibles. www.collectibles.about.com/library/weekly/aa080800a.html

"Limoges Box." La Boutique de la Porcelaine-Beware of Imitations. www.limoges-porcelains.com/pop/pop_imitation.php?param_langue=1+param_ses

"Limoges Box History." www.limogeshingedbox.com/admin/history.htm.

"The Manufacturing Process." www.ilimoges.com/process

"Old Paris Porcelain History." Antique China Porcelain & Collectibles. www.antique-china-porcelain-collectibles.com/old-paris-porcelain-history.html

"Samson Ceramics." Wikipedia, the Free Encyclopedia. www.en.wikipedia.org/wiki/samson_Ceramics

Index

Index